US & OUR PLANE

THIS

IS

EDITED BY
MAISIE SKIDMORE

HOW

WE

LIVE

US

&

OUR

PLANET

4

REST

5

PLAY

6

TOGETHERNESS

FOREWORD

IN 1976 OUR FATHER, Ingvar Kamprad, sat down with pen and paper and one intention: to set down the cornerstones of IKEA, the company he founded in 1943, and had already spent more than thirty years building. He wanted to capture its spirit, its culture and its values, so that they would be understood well into the future.

The result was *The Testament of a Furniture Dealer*, a short, simple text composed around our key values – from a willingness to make mistakes, to the power of collaboration. In nine points, he outlined our entire philosophy. 'Simplicity is a virtue,' he wrote in one chapter. In another: 'Waste of resources is one of the greatest diseases of mankind.' The most important of all our values, though, is togetherness – because IKEA is the work of many minds coming together, over the course of many years.

Perhaps most influential of all, Ingvar opened *The Testament* by outlining the IKEA vision – a call to action which remains our reason for existing today. 'To create a better everyday life for the many people,' it states. These words remain our most fundamental message.

Today, the battle that Ingvar fought in 1976 against the 'waste of resources' has taken on a new urgency, as the ecological crisis becomes a reality all around the world. Climate change is one of the greatest challenges that humanity faces. But 'a better everyday life for the many people' means having a positive impact on people *and* the planet. It means doing everything in our power to meet the needs of people today, without compromising the needs of future generations. It means optimism and action, and leading by example, which is why sustainability is at the top of our agenda.

By rethinking our own consumption and adopting new ways of working, we want IKEA to lead the way – together with our co-workers, customers and partners – in making a positive impact in environmental protection and regeneration. By 2030, we are determined to transform our way of working from linear to entirely circular; from using resources, to regenerating them. More importantly, in leading by example and demonstrating what is possible, we will inspire other companies to do the same.

As we write in 2021, IKEA has stores in more than sixty countries around the world. More than 220,000 co-workers breathe new life into his vision every day, redefining humbleness, willpower and 'making do' with every decision, every mistake, every delegation. This book is dedicated to all of our co-workers.

Ingvar's *Testament* demonstrates that there is great power in writing things down. To change the world, good ideas must be nurtured and magnified to reach as many people as possible. This book shows how inspiring people and their ideas can be.

But even more important than talk is action. As Ingvar said, 'whatever we are doing today, we can do a bit better tomorrow.' Through these pages, we hope to shine a light on some of the small things we can all do at home to have a positive impact on our planet. Together, we can all create 'a better everyday life for more of the many people.'

PETER, MATHIAS AND JONAS KAMPRAD

INTRODUCTION

ONCE AN AFTERTHOUGHT, sustainability has become a soft hum that underpins the soundtrack of our daily lives. The term is imperfect, of course. It attempts, somewhat clumsily, to refer to a whole raft of ideas, from consciousness, coexistence and responsibility to honesty, respect and action. Sustainability implies an Arcadian state in which all our systems are circular, our behaviours carefully considered and our planet unspoiled. And yet a future without a higher measure of it than we currently know is almost too catastrophic to comprehend: a world of drowned cities, burned forests and climate refugees. Sustainability is imperfect, but it's what we have. And so, we work with it.

Perhaps it comes momentarily to mind when you turn off the tap while brushing your teeth, unlock your bike to cycle to work or separate out your organic waste for composting. These small, everyday actions can feel inconsequential – especially when contrasted with the complex knots of governmental policy, or the extravagance of industry – but added up together, they amount to an extraordinary impact. They demonstrate our alignment in an ongoing conversation about the need to do more, and what that 'doing' looks like. The key is in togetherness. This is the way we change the world.

This is also the way we live our lives – through an ongoing and always evolving series of habits, ideas, insights and connections. Life, we understand, is about living, and all the small activities we each undertake every day in the pursuit of happiness. Naturally, other ideas get in the way; the things we value often are not the things that are the most valuable. In making this book, we decided to take a step back and try to glimpse the bigger picture. We've set out to think about the future of our planet through six of our most precious resources: time, space, food, rest, play and togetherness.

While stepping back, we also took many steps forwards – through doorways, porches, gates and onto boats from Mexico to Moscow, Bali to Beirut. Ever since the 1950s, IKEA has conducted Home Visits all over the world to find out more about the way people live. Inspired by the rigour, candour, curiosity and surprise that come with this approach, we visited twelve individuals and families around the world to find out about their own journey towards a more sustainable way of living. They are activists, artists, athletes, architects and entrepreneurs. Some take care of young children, some take care of forests. They shared ideas about the way we build our homes, move through our cities and clothe ourselves. Needless to say, we had something to learn from each one.

Among other things, we learned that home today isn't as simple a concept as it once was – particularly after the complex shift triggered by a global pandemic. We are at home in our gardens, our workplaces, our local parks, our markets and coffee shops. We make ourselves at home when we visit friends and neighbours, or take trips to new places. We build homes by connecting with others in our communities, feeding our local ecosystems and looking out for one another. So, we call our case studies not Home Visits, but Life Visits. They were conducted wherever possible by writers and photographers who live locally, minimizing unnecessary travel and resulting in an extraordinary cast of global contributors (find them on pages 250–1). In the interviews and images that follow, we hope to share just a small shred of what makes the life of each of our subjects – each of us – extraordinary. If they inspire an action that might make our world a little more sustainable, even better.

We have also considered the products that have epitomized IKEA's ideas about what makes 'good design' over the past seventy-odd years. Our Icons – each one a sustainable solution to either time, space, food, rest, play or togetherness – are inspired by the five dimensions of Democratic Design. This system was created by IKEA to aid it in developing products which 'the many people' both love and can afford; in order to be classified as Democratic Design, a product must check five boxes – form, function, quality, sustainability and low price. Taken together, our Icons make up just a small selection of the objects that have emerged from this rigorous design process. They continue to inform a range that includes beautiful, meaningful, long-lasting and affordable solutions to everyday problems, with a positive impact on people, society and our planet.

The Icons were developed out of in-depth research, rooted in real life. With this in mind, in our Rituals we investigate the nitty-gritty of the routines that shape our every day, and the objects and ideas that make those routines possible. Finally, through the Photo Essays, we invite artists and photographers to respond to our themes – which they do in original, mischievous and eccentric ways.

You could think of the book, as we have, as a research document of sorts. A study of sustainability – with everything that this term means – and how we live today. These stories have inspired us to make changes, big and small. We hope they do the same for you.

MAISIE SKIDMORE

TIME

IN A CONTEMPORARY world defined by the way we use and misuse resources, time remains the most precious of all. After all, it's the only currency which, once spent, can never be returned to us. In the battle against rising temperatures and the devastating impact climate change is already having around the world, time is not only important, it is crucial. Simply put: the sooner we change the way we live in the world, the better our chance to ensure it is safe and habitable for future generations.

Time has always been a concern for IKEA, whose raison d'être is to bring highly functional, well-made, long-lasting and sustainable design to many people at affordable prices. In this chapter's Icons, we consider how one beautifully made chair from the late 1970s is passing from hand to hand, as beloved now as it was almost fifty years ago.

Today, IKEA's interrogation of time culminates in one solution: circular design. Two products which have gone some way to helping the company on its quest to become 100 per cent circular by 2030: a modular storage system, designed to grow and adapt as you do; and the smart new joinery technique allowing customers to snap furniture together – and, crucially, apart again – in just moments.

Ridhima Pandey, a young environmental activist who lives in Uttarakhand, India, is forcefully aware of the ticking clock. When she was just nine years old she filed a petition against the Indian government with the National Green Tribunal, and later the Supreme Court of India, asserting that the Indian government had failed to fulfil its duties with regards to climate change. In her fourteen years on the planet, Ridhima has already done so much to prolong our existence on it.

In our changing relationship to the objects we own, craftsmanship is key. For Elora Hardy, the Bali-based designer imagining magical spaces inspired by nature and built (often) with bamboo, sustainability underpins everything: if an object is not good for the earth, it's not good for us. By designing structures that are made to last using this spectacularly fast-growing crop, and inspiring others to do the same, she is one of many building a future of hope and abundance for our children, and their children.

Finally, artist and image-maker Barbara Probst takes on time by reimagining an iconic scene from Alain Resnais's 1961 cult classic *Last Year at Marienbad*. Hers is a temporal experiment; in her hands, the camera becomes a time machine, exploding the moment and freezing it for posterity.

NATURA

IVAR

LISABO

Design by Karin Mobring, 1977

NATURA The most beautiful, well-crafted furniture designs are made with longevity in mind. They are intended to be handed down through generations, accruing emotional value along the way, and often garner historic status, selling at auction long after they were made.

This is certainly true of NATURA, a striking yet refined armchair in solid pine and tanned leather, launched in 1977. The sculptural seat was conceived by Swedish designer Karin Mobring and reflects the era's enduring appreciation for modernist furniture design with its emphasis on clean lines, exquisite craftsmanship and minimalist form.

The chair's title and use of sustainable wood and animal hide, meanwhile, indicate the design world's shift towards a more environmentally conscious approach in the latter half of the 1970s, following the plastic boom of the previous decade.

An instant classic, NATURA could soon be found in sitting rooms and studies around the world, serving as a contemporary, more compact alternative to traditional easy chairs.

With its covetable graphic silhouette, NATURA was always going to age well stylistically – in fact, it is now one of IKEA's most sought-after archive pieces – but thanks to its sturdy, lacquered-pine frame and durable leather seat, which softens and develops a pleasing patina over time, it is also able to withstand its popularity, long into the future.

Design by IKEA of Sweden, 1967

IVAR Often it's the simplest ideas that stand the test of time, as proved by IVAR, one of IKEA's most enduring icons of Democratic Design. The simple, customizable storage system has been a household staple for over half a century – although it's undergone a few name changes – and is widely deemed the piece that popularized unfinished pine in European interiors.

It originated in the late 1960s, when Ingvar Kamprad decided to implement knotty pine at IKEA for its abundance and affordability. Just then, IKEA's head of purchasing Lasse Olsson found himself drawn to the utilitarian pine shelves occupying many Swedish state buildings. But it was a young home furnishing specialist named Lennart Ekmark who put IVAR on the map, when he placed one of Lasse's prototypes in the living room section of IKEA's showroom.

Encapsulating the IKEA spirit of trial and error, it proved a surprise hit, coinciding with the new trend for 'pop furniture' that reflected the era's embrace of more casual modes of living. IVAR joined the IKEA range in 1967 and never left, its winning combination of low cost, simple construction, practicality and adaptability making it a universally popular design.

It is timeless in every sense: its raw materials are wholly sustainable (even its joints are wooden offcuts rescued during production); its solid pine is 'essentially impossible to wear out' to quote Lennart himself; while its modularity makes it easy and inexpensive to adapt, upgrade and repair – the epitome of circular design.

Moreover, IVAR can be customized over and over again, via the many combinations of components and accessories available to play with. It can be built upwards or outwards to fill any space; bottle racks added for the kitchen or cabinets for the study; and the untreated pine painted or stained any shade.

Design by Knut Hagberg and Marianne Hagberg, 2015

LISABO Time savers are invaluable, and the LISABO table collection, whose long solid birch legs and elegant ash-veneered beech top fit together in a snap, is no exception.

The secret to the table's quick assembly is a joint called the Wedge Dowel, conceived in the IKEA Prototype Shop by engineers Anders Eriksson and Göran Sjöstedt. The invisible fitting's machine-milled grooves click into corresponding pre-drilled holes, removing the need for screws, bolts and additional tools: a remarkable breakthrough in circular design.

Brother-sister design duo Knut and Marianne Hagberg, who first discovered the Wedge Dowel, put it to use in a series of light, contemporary tables they were devising. It soon revealed its potential to revolutionize flatpack furniture design and reduce assembly time by up to eighty per cent.

The Hagbergs incorporated the fitting into the leg design, allowing the legs to insert directly into the tabletop and lock into place in seconds. This had the dual purpose of making the table extremely durable, without detracting from its graceful appearance and handcrafted feel.

Just like that, the LISABO was born. The range went on to scoop a prestigious Red Dot Design Award in 2016 for its modern aesthetic and technological innovation, before it even hit the shelves.

One of the best-loved things about this collection of tables is that they are as quick to take apart as they are to put together and, unlike pieces held together by screws, remain just as robust after being reassembled.

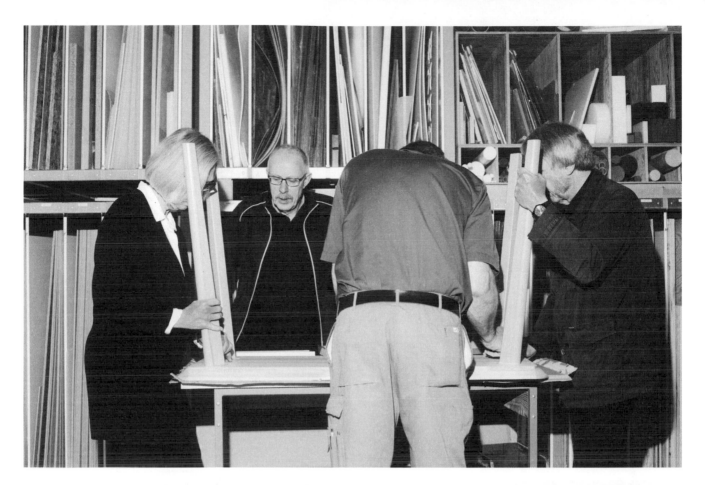

ELORA

HARDY

TIME

LIKE BAMBOO, Elora Hardy's way of moving through the world is at once childish and spontaneous, calm and resilient. And she knows the material well: as the founder and creative director of IBUKU, she leads an architecture and design firm that uses bamboo to create mesmerizing buildings on her home island of Bali, Indonesia, and around the world.

She was born in Canada and raised in Bali – where her father, the irrepressible John Hardy, was to co-found The Green School with his wife Cynthia – and moved to the USA at the age of fourteen. She went on to study Fine Arts in New York, before spending twelve years building a career in fashion. But as a daughter of Indonesia, who speaks Bahasa with the babbling dexterity of a Balinese flower seller, Elora was drawn back to Indonesia to discover and follow her passion: building sustainable structures out of bamboo. Now, she and the IBUKU team work tirelessly to bring some lush tropical sense to a parched, urbanized world.

As the parents of two feisty 'tropical' children, Nayan and Nusa, she and her husband Rajiv have converted a fancy bamboo bunk bed into a rustic tree house, beyond which an overgrown garden flourishes with impetuous blossoms and crotchety bugs.

BT: What is it about life in Bali that drew you back here?

EH: I felt distanced from the creative process when I was working in New York. It's the dialogue with craftspeople that brings the interconnectedness between people and product. Even in my art school, the learning was very isolating, and I ran away from that.

For me, working with creative people is about engagement, co-creation and teamwork. I certainly feel more connected to nature in Bali, and I am most comfortable creating here.

BT: What does sustainability mean to you?

EH: As a teenager I was always curious about why things were being made in a certain way and what purpose they served. I understood that the resources we used to build would not be acceptable in the coming decade.

A pivotal moment came when I watched a documentary by architect William McDonough, called *The Next Industrial Revolution*. This documentary had a huge impact on me, because I realized it wasn't coming from a restricted place of 'reduce, refuse, reuse,' or the constraints of simply using less. In fact, what McDonough said is that the 'question before us is not growth versus no growth. It is: what would good growth look like? And this is a question of intent, of design.'

Words BANDANA TEWARI
Photography THOMAS SITO

This made me think about designing differently, designing *out* waste, creating loops instead of downward spirals. He shifted my perspective. Sustainability itself is mislabelled. There are fun and creative possibilities.

BT: **How did you come to work with bamboo?**

EH: Bamboo is a remarkable renewable resource, which grows abundantly in Indonesia. It regenerates over a short period, it's flexible, malleable, and its compressive force is as strong as concrete, which is astounding. There is also no plant in nature that can grow as fast, producing as much as one metre in a day. While we know that this endless harvest is bountiful, we have learned that bamboo cannot be constrained. We had to reimagine our architectural discourse.

IBUKU was inspired by my father, John Hardy, and his wife Cynthia, the co-founders of the Green School, and their dream to nurture children while enveloped in a space that would be beautiful, respectful of the natural landscape and filled with hope for a bountiful future. Bamboo was by far the cleanest resource to use.

BT: **What inspires you?**

EH: Simply watching local women weaving prayer offerings out of palm leaves galvanized my passion. Art in the Western world is often confined to a conversation between a specific group and a gallery space. The word 'art' doesn't really apply to the Balinese way of life that I know and love. The beauty of art, design and ritual were not part of my Western education. I understand now that in Bali, it's not beauty for beauty's sake; beauty is intrinsically tied to design and function.

BT: **How has IBUKU evolved since it was founded eleven years ago?**

EH: While our architectural focus started on the dynamic bamboo structural shells, as we got deeper, we realized that the interiors had to live up to the impressive outer structures. Small details like doorknobs and railings, which wouldn't have raised much attention in regular buildings, look incongruous against bamboo, if not thoughtfully designed. Every mundane detail has to fit

into the architectural narrative. But that's where it gets exciting. We use leftover bamboo to create special features. We keep an eye out for the most freaky 'outlier' bamboos every time we get a fresh batch, because they invite us to look at bamboo differently again and again.

BT: What are the small things we can all do to have less of an impact on our environment?

EH: On a day-to-day level, people can make good long-term choices for the things they bring into their homes. Convenience and instant gratification undermine our long-term health. If we can make choices for our own future comfort, and invest in long-lasting things, that shifts everything.

For someone like me, attached to beauty and quality, it is tempting to buy objects that look good, but aren't *made* good. Beauty only matters when it supports Earth as our home forever. It's not enough to be 'better' or create 'less' harm – we need ways to be good, be proud of what we do and make. That's part of what the circular economy strives for.

BT: How do you relax together as a family?

EH: Right now our recreation revolves around our two children. We built a little tree house from scraps of bamboo patched together; we have been delighted at the sight of seeing our son Nayan swinging on a guava tree that is currently just right for his height.

BT: How does your day change with the seasons?

EH: In the dry season in Bali we have a routine of going down to the river in the late afternoons. Nusa, my daughter, and her nanny go to the fresh water spring by the river, almost every day. And of course, cooking together as a family is always delightful.

'It's not enough to be "better" or create "less" harm – we need ways to be good, be proud of what we do and make.'

— ELORA HARDY

Ritual:
Elora Hardy nurses her daughter at sunrise and sunset

LIFE WITH SMALL children tends to be structured around a diverse and ever-evolving series of routines and rituals. At sunrise and sunset, Elora Hardy curls up on a curved bamboo sofa to nurse her daughter, Nusa. Rays of sun filter through the verdant trees outside, dappling them with light as they sit quietly together.

The sofa, with its simple and voluptuous silhouette, was designed explicitly for the corner of the home that houses it. Its surface is covered with a smattering of cushions made from handmade textiles Elora gathered over the course of many years, while its curving bamboo form twists in on itself, 'and kind of hugs you,' Elora says. 'Like a comforting embrace.'

The piece was created with comfort and calm in mind. 'When you flop on it, the view transports you,' she continues. 'Your gaze drifts into the distant horizon of towering trees. That point of view is very relaxing to the human eye, because, as we know now, the unfocused gaze into the distance causes the least amount of stress to the eyes.'

It also allows Elora a moment to look out over their untamed garden and to the forest beyond it. It's a view she is thankful for. 'I remember when I was in New York,' she says, 'it was my aspiration to have an apartment where a window looked out to a tree and a little piece of the sky.' In that concrete jungle, however, 'it was remarkably difficult!'

Now, of course, she has swapped out concrete and steel for close proximity to a real jungle. Ordinary though it is, the familiar and habitual act of dropping languidly onto a sofa to feed her baby allows Elora a moment of gratitude for the many blessings she and her family have been bestowed with.

Words BANDANA TEWARI
Photography THOMAS SITO

Photo Essay: Barbara Probst

ALAIN RESNAIS'S 1961 film *Last Year at Marienbad* is a fragmented study of memory and perception. Two people meet in a baroque hotel. The man claims they fell in love there one year prior; the woman insists she doesn't remember. Here, Barbara Probst recreates the film's most iconic scene: a sprawling view of the hotel's garden, dotted with statues and static figures. Activating multiple cameras simultaneously, Barbara slices into the tableau to offer a multidimensional impression of one moment in time – frozen, splintered and preserved for posterity.

RIDHIMA PANDEY'S BEDROOM is simple, charming and fun. Handmade paper crafts and stickers decorate her walls and cupboards. A bright red desk smiles at all who enter. On her bed, three tabby cats, Miya, Tiger and Dodo, cosy up on a pillow. 'I liked it when everyone gathered around here to watch the TV I had in my room,' she says, referring to her parents, both environmentalists, and her younger brother. 'Now, we've moved it to the living room.'

The fourteen-year-old has grown up here, in Haridwar, an ancient city and much-visited Hindu pilgrimage site in Uttarakhand, northern India. The town is located on the banks of the Ganges, which emerges from the Himalayas – but Ridhima has a conflicted relationship with the river. 'I enjoy calm waters,' she explains. Understandably so; when she was seven, she witnessed a deadly flash flood that swept across the state, destroying families and property. 'At that time, I didn't understand any big concepts,' she explains. 'The only thing I knew was that flash floods existed, and that I could lose my parents to one.'

Compelled to do whatever she could to ease the crisis that caused such floods, she filed a petition in the National Green Tribunal in 2017 noting the government's pointed lack of action over the climate crisis. The petition was dismissed, but she has since taken it to the country's Supreme Court. At the same time, she leads community efforts to plant trees, campaigns widely to protect animals and speaks to politicians and changemakers all over the world. At home in Haridwar and further afield, Ridhima's gentle, grassroots activism is turning ripples into waves.

GR: **What inspired you to take up climate activism?**

RP: It wasn't inspiration really, but fear that pushed me in this direction. The 2013 Kedarnath flash floods were devastating. It impacted many kids, including me. After having nightmares for a long time, I made up my mind to do something about it.

GR: **How did you go about connecting the dots?**

RP: This is how my mum explained global warming to me. She said, 'Imagine the Earth cooking under a fire. The temperature will increase and the fire will grow more and more intense because of rising carbon emissions.' I was confused. Even if the temperature was rising, how could it be bad? I used to love summers, so it made me want to learn more. Funnily, when my dad said that I would be most affected by climate change, I took it too personally. I didn't realize he was talking about my whole generation. I thought, 'why only me!'

Words GAUTAMI REDDY
Photography DEVASHISH GAUR

My first decision was to live a sustainable life.

GR: What does it mean to live more sustainably?

RP: The idea was to prevent rising temperatures that are causing glaciers to melt and flood downstream. I started by saving electricity, water, food and paper. I stopped using plastic or buying packaged products. I carry my own cloth bags, water bottle and cutlery when I go out. I go to the local market instead of shopping online and rely on my bicycle and public transport whenever possible, or simply walk the distance. It's also our family ritual to plant saplings and trees on birthdays and festivals. Oh, and I love wearing my mum's old clothes. Every time she buys a new kurta or sari, I tell her that she must pass it on to me in a few years. I have to trim and cut a few, but they fit me perfectly.

GR: What's the point of petitioning?

RP: Initially, I thought living a sustainable life could bring about sufficient change, and that it could even stop flash floods! But I realized that it is hardly enough.

I needed to do something bigger, and that's when I decided to petition against the Indian government for not taking climate change seriously. It was a means to start a dialogue. Recently, along with sixteen other children, I also filed a petition to move the United Nations against climate inaction.

GR: Young activists are on the rise. Do you think world leaders are paying attention?

RP: The older generation is so occupied with speaking their own agenda. We are invited to events, meets and conferences, but we hardly get to speak. They say they want to work with us, but when we share our thoughts, there is no response. It's like they're saying, 'You're doing a great job, and now you can leave!' It would do more good if people actually sat and listened to what we have to say.

GR: What's most special about young activists?

RP: We take it seriously. We don't run a company, government or a business. We don't have profits to lose

– only our future. Seeing the older generation not paying attention, we are taking charge.

GR: Do you have a personal slogan or mantra?

RP: As Gandhi said, 'Be the change that you wish to see in the world.' I feel that if you truly want to bring about change, the ideas will come to mind. If you feel the need to do something, the brain will automatically think of solutions, big and small.

GR: What advice would you give to kids hoping to make a difference?

RP: Start by doing it yourself. And strike! It is within your right to do so, especially if you feel that you have been wronged in some way. Strikes give people context. It is a space for learning, for children and adults.

GR: Is there a place for failure in activism?

RP: Oh, plenty. Things don't go as planned, they never do. Initially, I didn't know if the government had read my petition, but now that we are campaigning and involving the community, we know they are listening. At the same time, in some of the clean-up and planting drives that I organize around the neighbourhood, no one turns up except my best friend! Sometimes you have to do it yourself.

GR: What's your plant collection like?

RP: I love indoor plants, but the cats often damage them. My brother and I picked a few potted plants for our balcony though. There's also a little kitchen garden outside my house, where my dad grows all the simple, 'practical' plants, from chilli and lemon to rose and lemongrass. Right across from that is a line of trees and saplings that I sowed. My favourite is an Ashoka tree. I planted it on Earth Day a couple of years ago, it's grown so tall and good-looking.

'We don't run a company, government or a business. We don't have profits to lose – only our future. Seeing the older generation not paying attention, we are taking charge.'

— RIDHIMA PANDEY

GR: What's your favourite place at home?

RP: Right here, at my study desk. It is where I do my homework, meetings and online classes.

GR: What do you say to those who don't believe in climate change?

RP: I doubt they're informed!

SPACE

AS THE NUMBER of people on the planet increases and urban populations grow denser, our homes are – necessarily – shrinking. Houses become flats, become studio apartments in high-rise blocks. Families relocate to narrowboats, camper vans and tiny houses. In spaces like these, three-dimensional thinking triumphs. Organization becomes crucial. Wasting valuable space in an inner-city home seems careless; we need it, after all, for playing, dancing and living in. In our new age of both less and more, we can all learn to buy fewer things, and use them better.

IKEA is an expert in this – entrusted around the world for its affordable, sustainable solutions to small-space living. In this chapter, our icons consider three pivotal pieces: a very early example of flatpack furniture, easily constructed, for economy and ease in delivery; a sofa bed designed for multifunction, minimalism and a nomadic way of life; and one of the company's beloved step stools, which makes cubic metres as accessible as square ones.

But outside of the city, space isn't always at a premium; Midori Shintani is one person with plenty of it. As the head gardener of the Tokachi Millennium Forest, a vast, visionary environmental project located on Japan's northernmost island, she tends to 400 hectares (988 acres) day in, day out, safeguarding its 1000-year vision. This vast expanse of woodland was founded by entrepreneur Mitsushige Hayashi to offset the carbon footprint of his national newspaper business. In the meantime, it offers Japan's urban population a precious opportunity to commune with nature through its gardens, farms and forests. There they can access a wealth of space, however little they may have at home.

At the other end of the spectrum, we meet the Leven family, whose apartment just outside Moscow shape-shifts to accommodate young family life in all its forms. This compact space functions in several different ways at once – and does so admirably, evolving with its inhabitants. For them, as for so many around the world, living more responsibly is a daily endeavour; they share some of their acquired wisdom in the pages that follow.

Artist and image-maker Liam Sielski Waters, meanwhile, reimagines space in its most abstract and unlimited form – a fantasy CGI landscape of concrete architectural objects that coexist with nature. He depicts a symbiotic relationship as tangible as it is surreal. Whether his invented world is a post-apocalyptic scene – the aftermath of the climate crisis, perhaps – or a picture of a harmonious coexistence between human beings and nature, is for its viewer to decide.

LÖVET

IKEA PS SOFA BED

BEKVÄM

Design by IKEA of Sweden, 1956

LÖVET Throughout IKEA's history, problems have served as a catalyst for innovation. If Gillis Lundgren, the first marketing director, hadn't struggled to fit an early IKEA coffee table into the trunk of his car, the company might look very different today.

The table was a sample of LÖVET, a mid-century side table with a leaf-shaped jacaranda top and three solid beech legs. It was 1955, and Gillis was tasked with driving the table from a furniture-maker's workshop in rural Sweden to a catalogue photo shoot at the IKEA headquarters.

Realizing there wasn't enough space for the LÖVET in the back of his station wagon, he decided to saw the table's legs off and reattach them upon his arrival. It struck him then that breaking down furniture into parts that could be self-assembled would make the designs both easier to transport and more affordable.

Inspired, he took the idea back to Ingvar Kamprad, convincing him to establish build-it-yourself furniture as the foundation of the IKEA business model. LÖVET was launched in 1956 as one of IKEA's first flatpack designs, kickstarting a ready-to-assemble furniture revolution.

With its seminal history and sophisticated but playful modernist form, LÖVET would go on to become a treasured icon in the IKEA archive, frequently sought after at auction. So, when Ingvar suggested remaking a series of classic IKEA furniture from the 1950s and 60s in 2013, LÖVET was high on the list.

The new design was almost identical, except for its name, LÖVBACKEN, and the use of poplar veneer instead of jacaranda as a more sustainable option for the tabletop. Today, it remains a favourite piece in the IKEA range, imbued with the storied past of its predecessor.

IKEA PS SOFA BED As the world's cities have grown, our homes, by necessity, have shrunk, causing us to rely more than ever on furniture to expand our rooms' functions. A dexterous desk may double as a dining table, while a sofa bed can turn a sitting room into a bedroom in moments.

The IKEA PS SOFA BED, designed by Chris Martin and Thomas Sandell, and launched in 1999, is one such item. An armless two-seater couch with down cushions that double as pillows, its simple appearance belies its clever design. With a sharp tug, the steel-framed sofa rolls out smoothly into a double bed, courtesy of its front wheels, whose large size allows them to glide with such ease that it can even be manipulated with one hand.

The sofa bed formed part of IKEA's second IKEA PS collection, a recurring series that invites designers to interpret a specific theme with the aim of developing Scandinavian design in innovative and affordable ways. This collection centred on small-space living – multifunctional and flexible pieces that left as much space as possible for other activities.

Uniquely, customers could choose from three types of mattresses when making their purchase, as well as a selection of removable fabric covers. Meanwhile, an optional matching storage box, which slid beneath the couch, placed bedding within easy reach.

Design by Chris Martin and Thomas Sandell, 1999

BEKVÄM When it comes to maximizing indoor storage space, often the only way is up. But hiding things up high tends to place them out of reach, creating a new point of contention.

The BEKVÄM step stool, designed by long-standing IKEA designer Nike Karlsson, was launched in 2000, providing a convenient and low-cost leg-up.

Originally produced in aspen but now made in solid birch or beech, the sturdy and refined design was intended to provide the simplest possible solution to the problem at hand. The legs are slanted and proportioned to support the stool's two rectangular steps, while the hole in the top step serves as a handle.

Simple though it is, the BEKVÄM has a shapely appeal and a strong enough character to look purposeful even when not in use. At 50-centimetres tall (almost 20-inches tall) the stool is slightly higher than a regular chair, making it deliberately multifunctional; young children can happily use it as a high stool, perching on top, with their feet resting on the bottom step, while adults can move it from place to place, to access out-of-reach hideaways.

But beyond these conventional uses, its designer has seen it repurposed as a bedside table, a plant stand, a fixture in horse stables and much more. The solid wood finish, meanwhile, lends it to decoration and customization.

Design by Nike Karlsson, 2000

MIDORI

SHINTANI

SITUATED IN THE far reaches of the northernmost island in the Japanese archipelago, Tokachi Millennium Forest is a place unlike any other. It was first created as part of one visionary publisher's mission to offset the carbon produced by his newspaper business, and to create 'a garden for a thousand years' for future generations to enjoy.

From its position in the foothills of the Hidaka Mountains, this vast and profound space of 400 hectares (988 acres) – which reaches lows of -25 degrees Celsius in winter – comprises forests, gardens, farms and a café, where visitors can eat from plants that grow naturally in the grounds. The forest also provides a vital point of contact with the natural world for Japan's large urban population. With its naturalistic landscape design and thoughtful combinations of native plants and perennials, the site, which follows the ancient Japanese calendar of seventy-two seasons and is inspired by the Japanese term *satoyama*, or the coexistence of humans with nature, is a world of its own.

Since 2008, head gardener Midori Shintani has led the team there alongside landscape designer Dan Pearson, merging a 'new Japanese horticulture' with Hokkaido's wild nature. With her irrepressible passion, she oversees the landscape's vast grounds, tools in hand, allowing it to thrive by simply letting nature lead the way. We met her there, and sat down to talk in the gardener's cottage she often occupies during her days in the grounds.

JK: **How did the Tokachi Millennium Forest come about? What drew you to it?**

MS: Hokkaido has always been a land of pioneers. Our owner, newspaper publisher Mitsushige Hayashi, purchased a formerly abandoned site to create an environmental conservation project, intended to offset the carbon created by his business. In 1996 he enlisted landscape architect Fumiaki Takano of Takano Landscape Planning to develop a site masterplan for a new public garden. Garden designer Dan Pearson joined in 2000, and developed the idea of naturalistic planting with cultivated gardening. In 2007, when I saw that the Millennium Forest had announced a job opportunity, I knew that I should go.

JK: **How do you choose which plants to introduce?**

MS: Dan and I are always discussing plants – not only native plants, but cultivars. We merge Japanese native and North American species, because we have a similar climate, and also the garden cultivars, and then mingle them in the garden. We feel it's our mission to

Words JOANNA KAWECKI
Photography TAKASHI HOMMA

introduce new plants, because there are so many great plants on Earth! We like to introduce something new to the visitors. Because meeting plants is the most joyful part of gardening, and the garden.

JK: **Your team is small, with only two full-time gardeners. How do you decide where to focus your energy?**

MS: Plants and the garden are always our first priority. We want to support the plants in their growth. Because humans cannot live without plants; that's what I always teach young gardeners or students. As gardeners, I think we have a responsibility to touch nature. So, once I commit, or put my hands in it, I hope to have developed the strong will to continue that, because my hands are connected to the future landscape.

Tokachi Millennium Forest's mission is to preserve a rich, natural environment for future generations. But at the same time, there is another message. We humans think about 100 years at a time. But as a part of nature, we should think about 1,000 years – the forest's time, not our own time. Ours is just a tiny, tiny, little piece of time, in the huge 1,000-year forest history, but it has an impact.

JK: **What is your daily schedule like?**

MS: It is always changing, based on the climate, from sunny days to rainy days. The native vegetation is always changing by itself, but we put our hands on it in very humble ways to make a beautiful balance. We use a lot of herbs or mountain vegetables, and when we use native plants – say, a very vigorous one, like Japanese knotweed – we harvest and use them as food at the garden café. So, it is very similar to our ancestors living in *satoyama* [the geographic area between a village and the foothills of a mountain, where villagers have coexisted with nature for centuries].

JK: **Do you have a favourite season in the garden?**

MS: I actually like the beginning of the garden season in April, once the native vegetation has started germinating again. I feel a deep happiness, because it has survived a long, harsh winter, and then I can eventually meet the plants again. It's quite a magical moment for me to witness this in the forest. Once the snow starts to melt, I'm just staring at the forest floor, waiting for the plants to come out again. I can hardly wait. Every year, it's quite dramatic.

JK: How might we all spend more time with nature?

MS: You can live with plants in many ways. I cut flowers almost every day, that's one part of our lifestyle. Once you cut a flower, you might find another perspective that also provides a closer relationship with plants. Originally, *ikebana* [traditional Japanese flower arrangement] originated from showing our respect to nature. A kind of devotion to nature is in our DNA, you could say. There is one idea I love from the tea master Sen no Rikyū, who created the ten rules of the tea ceremony, to arrange the flower like a bay leaf in a field. If you cut flowers or plants and decorate with them at home, you bring one aspect of nature in. I really love that.

JK: What do you hope for visitors to the forest to take away with them?

MS: Tokachi Millennium Forest is a great place to realize that we are part of nature. That's the most important message – the garden is like a bridge connecting us to the nature beyond. I hope our visitors realize that, and gain happiness and comfort from it. It's not something to be afraid of, you know? Then we are able to see what we have to do. That's the whole theme of the project: how we carry on this rich biodiversity for future generations. Millennium Forest is a kind of hope, designed to show that we can preserve, or live with, a beautiful, rich, natural environment for a long, long time.

'Meeting plants is the most joyful part of gardening'

— **MIDORI SHINTANI**

Ritual:
Midori Shintani serves tea to visiting guests

'**JAPANESE PEOPLE PUT** an emphasis on hospitality,' explains Midori Shintani, looking over her carefully laid table at the traditional thatched cottage she spends time in during her days in the forest. In fact, the Japanese term, *omotenashi*, which translates loosely as 'wholeheartedly looking after guests' goes above and beyond hospitality – it denotes an attention to even the smallest detail. 'For anyone who comes to the Millennium Forest, I like to create a strong connection between them and nature, and plants.'

When Dan Pearson, the forest's landscape designer, other gardeners or friends from foreign countries visit, Midori organizes tea time together. 'Sometimes it is just a very simple green tea,' she explains. 'I usually set up my tea time table in the corner of the Garden Café for guests, and use my favourite tools. I bring my cast-iron *tetsubin* teapot and my ceramics.'

These ceramics are particularly special. 'They were passed down from my grandmother and grandfather. My grandfather loved Japanese culture – he also held tea ceremonies and made a garden – and was a huge inspiration for me,' says Midori. 'My grandparent's house in the area of Seto near Aichi Prefecture is also famous for its Seto ware, where my ceramics are from. The teapot is my favourite. It is Nambu ironware.'

Her favourite ironware maker is called Kamasada. 'I usually bring that teapot, which is very heavy, when Dan or other guests visit,' she says. 'I set the table and decorate with flowers, and we use a big leaf,' – either Magnolia obovata or Japanese knotweed – 'from the garden in the forest as a big plate.'

'That is one element of our direct connection with plants,' she continues. 'The garden is not only a place to show beautiful flowers, but a place where we experience the living landscape. Then to bring that experience back to the home, and make it part of our lifestyle, that's what I hope to share with visitors, through the garden.'

Words JOANNA KAWECKI
Photography TAKASHI HOMMA

Photo Essay:
Liam Sielski Waters

ENTER AN ILLUSORY world where wild, organic forms grow up through, over and around towering concrete structures, and a soft light bathes the abandoned relics of everyday existence. In this series of computer-generated images, Liam Sielski Waters approaches space as an abstract concept, blurring the boundaries between familiarity and fantasy, natural and man-made, architecture and arcadia, to create something much more surreal.

THE LEVEN

FAMILY

MARK AND LENA Leven and their young son Daniel live in the bustling, industrial city of Khimki, near Moscow. A graphic designer and an interior designer respectively, the couple met through work ten years ago. They connected over a love of design, centred around sustainability and minimalism. An exploration of their 42-square-metre (452-square-foot) home, in a modern apartment block overlooking a playground and a crop of other high-rise buildings, reveals all you need to know about the couple's conscious approach.

To step through the Levens' front door is to enter into a sanctuary of calm. A sea of white walls and oak-emulating PVC tiles form the backdrop to the fluid interior, punctuated by black, white and wooden furnishings. The hallway leads to the heart of the home: a living room-slash-play area, which gives way to a dining space and kitchen. Only the family's bathroom and bedroom lie behind closed doors.

Notable is the unexpected sense of space, the result of discreet storage systems, and the family's limiting of their possessions to what they need or treasure most. Curated trinkets, including Cambodian sculptures and a set of all-white matryoshkas, speak to the couple's appreciation for travel and their own Russian heritage, while the bunches of dried flowers and plethora of recycling containers dotted around the home convey their love of nature, and determination to protect it.

DW: **Mark and Lena, what drew you to each other?**

ML: We have a lot of the same interests: home furnishing – we're passionate about interior design and unique objects with a history   music and travel. We love to visit new places, usually mountains, forests, seas. We're less attracted to cities.

LL: We also shared the same vision for the future.

DW: **What was that?**

ML: A balance between enjoying the comforts of contemporary life and finding harmony with nature. It's very important for us to live sustainably; we appreciate minimalism and mindfulness – both at home, and in life generally.

DW: **Why did you choose to live in Khimki?**

ML: Two years ago, I accepted a new role based in Moscow, so we moved there from Novosibirsk, Siberia. We bought this apartment a year ago. Although Khimki is a busy city, we live in a quiet district. A lot of families live here. There are many parks, lots of nature; we

Words DAISY WOODWARD
Photography GUEORGUI PINKHASSOV

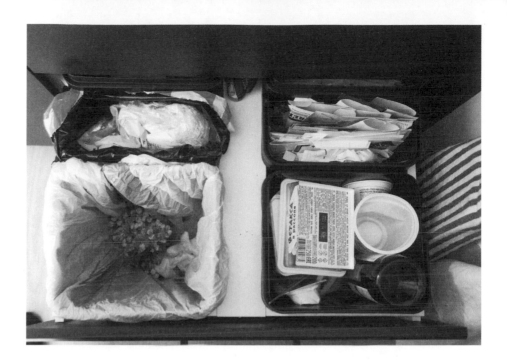

like to cycle here in the summer. We're very close to Moscow for work, which is a comfortable, modern city with so much to do. You can travel almost anywhere from there too.

DW: **Why did you opt for this particular apartment?**

ML: It was a brand new apartment, with no walls or furnishings, which allowed us to design everything from scratch to meet our personal needs.

DW: **How did you do this?**

ML: It's quite a small apartment, but with smart planning and a minimalist approach, we created a comfortable, aesthetically pleasing practical space that allows us to do all the activities we've always enjoyed. One of the secrets to this is creating multifunctional rooms. Our bedroom is also a home office and a sewing area for Lena, who makes her own clothes, and the kitchen, dining, living and play areas all exist in one space.

LL: That was important for us so that Daniel can be with us whenever he wants to be; he can cook with us in the kitchen, for example, or play nearby.

DW: **How did you achieve this multifunctionality and sense of fluidity?**

ML: Careful forethought – making sure everything is stored within easy reach – and the active use of white in the interior. White visually expands a small space and allows you to relax your eyes.

LL: We're surrounded by a lot of colour and complex visual elements at work, so we wanted a calming home environment. That's also very important for Daniel so he isn't over-stimulated.

DW: **What's your favourite part of the apartment, Daniel?**

DL: Wherever my toys are.

ML: He spends a lot of time in the bathroom. He recently learned to wash his hands, which he does about ten times a day.

LL: He loves to swim too. He's an Aquarius.

DW: **You've also incorporated a lot of black and wooden details throughout the apartment. Tell us about that.**

LL: Black and white because it's a classic combination. Then we integrated lots of natural, sustainable materials into the space – wood, rattan, wicker and natural fabrics like cotton – to create cosiness and connect us to nature.

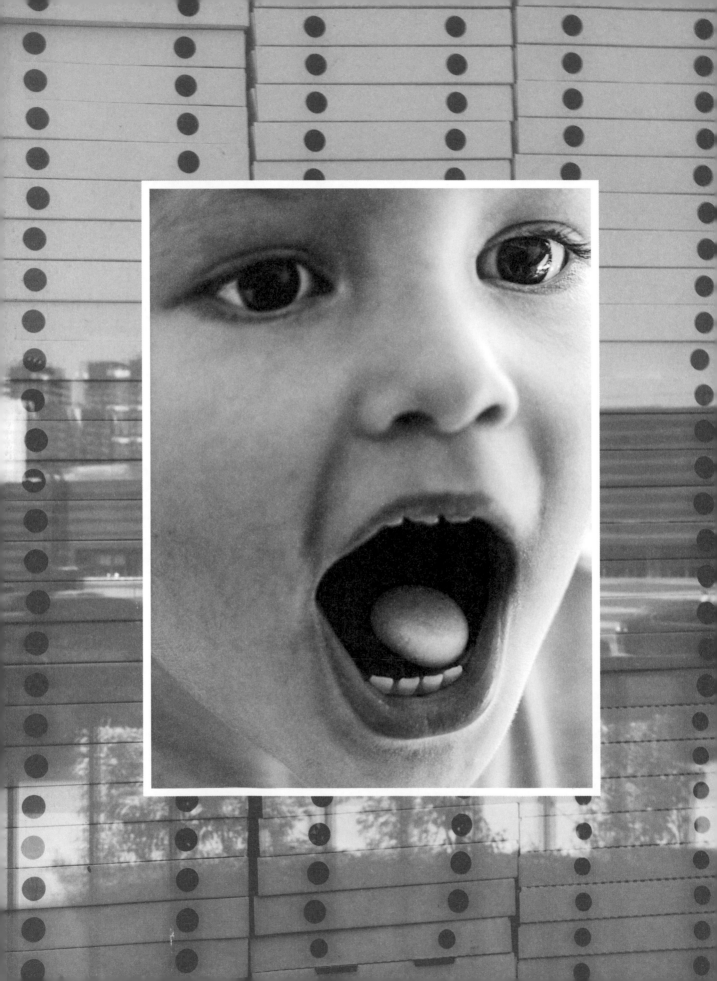

DW: Sustainability is clearly very important to you. Has that always been the case?

LL: Learning more about sustainability, when it became a mainstream topic, made us realize we needed to take action. Having a baby increased this desire. Living sustainably is vital for our children; we're building their future.

ML: Humans' negative impact upon nature is evident in even the wildest, most inaccessible places – something we've noticed while travelling. It's difficult to enjoy nature when you're surrounded by rubbish. Restructuring our way of life to become more eco-conscious was so natural and simple. Our next step is to inspire the people around us to do the same by demonstrating how easy it is to implement these small but important everyday changes.

DW: What are your tips for doing so?

LL: Reduce the number of objects in your life; think about what will happen to what you buy after you're gone. But keep your favourite things close by so you can appreciate them.

ML: Sort your waste, give up packaging and buy food products in your own containers. Carry reusable bags and a water bottle with you. Use natural materials in your home, and opt for durable and high-quality items. Embrace technological progress: a dishwasher or induction hob will save resources and free up time for what matters. And allow yourself to relax, especially in nature!

'Restructuring our way of life to become more eco-conscious was so natural and simple. Our next step is to inspire the people around us to do the same'

— MARK LEVEN

FOOD

IT'S BOTH PART of our cultural heritage and a source of enormous pleasure. But when you sit down to it three times a day – ready and available, delicious and nutritious – it's easy to forget how necessary food is to our survival.

Today, that's something we have no choice but to remain mindful of. Extreme weather conditions, water scarcity and threats to biodiversity are already threatening food production. It's a new reality we must learn to accommodate – and wherever possible, to ease.

Fortunately, small changes to our daily habits add up. Whether it's preparing more food at home, where the addition of fresh and locally grown fruit and vegetables to our daily diets proves excellent both for our individual health and that of our planet, or bringing food storage solutions to the fridge to help reduce household waste, we can all make modest improvements every day.

Our Icons celebrate some of IKEA's small-but-mighty innovations. Starting with food itself: the IKEA Restaurant and Bistro brought a plant-based alternative to the now iconic meatball to stores all around the world – at just four per cent of the climate footprint of the original. There's also a celebration of simple but innovative new ideas that keep leftovers fresher for longer, and the first comprehensive collection that allowed those moving out on their own for the very first time to build a kitchen to be proud of.

Some sustainable solutions to the way we eat are good for the soul too. From his home in South Central Los Angeles, an area he designates as a 'food prison', fashion designer-turned-activist Ron Finley launched a revolution: to make healthy and nutritious food available to his local population. A few vegetables planted in the unused verges in his neighbourhood quickly transformed into a global mission. Now he's using his ever-growing influence 'to plant seeds in your mind,' as he puts it, 'and let you harvest the fruit that grows.'

Both a social justice issue and its remedy, food has the power to bring us together. In Beirut, activist, entrepreneur and restaurateur Kamal Mouzawak altered the shape of food culture with the opening of Souk El Tayeb, the city's first weekly open-air farmer's market since the Civil War, and a long and ever-lengthening string of projects celebrating the true spirit of Lebanese cuisine. So, when his city was brought to its knees by a catastrophic explosion in August 2020, he set about healing it the way he knows best: by feeding it. He tells us the story from his Beirut apartment – the enduring impact of that now infamous day visible from his window.

Finally, photographer Matthew Donaldson shares a series that depicts food as you've never seen it before. A long-time advocate for experimentation, messiness and play, he celebrates the familiar 'oops' moment with a delectable study of colour, texture and form. A feast for the eyes, we think you'll agree.

STARTBOX
KÖK No.1

IKEA 365+

HUVUDROLL

Design by IKEA of Sweden, 1987

STARTBOX KÖK No.1 Decking out a first kitchen can be a daunting task and, in the 1980s, it was also an expensive one. In 1985, Ingvar Kamprad set out to democratize the cooking process for students and the newly independent alike, driven by a belief that making and enjoying home-made food is an essential rite of passage.

The STARTBOX KÖK No.1 launched two years later, a fifty-piece starter pack containing everything required to create a culinary hub. Designed by IKEA's in-house team including Knut and Marianne Hagberg, its contents ranged from pots and pans to spatulas and sieves through bottle openers and beyond.

There was also one radical inclusion: the garlic press, a special piece that stood out alongside all the kitchen basics, and went very much against the Swedish culinary tradition at the time. All the pieces were available to buy separately, but were considerably discounted when purchased together in the boldly branded cardboard STARTBOX KÖK No.1.

Although the collection was conceived as a low-cost launchpad for budding chefs, the overarching aim was that these objects – made from enduring materials like stainless steel and cast iron – should embody great, long-lasting design.

Quality and functionality were ensured through a rigorous system of tests carried out by an external company in Stockholm, and the STARTBOX KÖK No.1 proved a huge hit for years to come.

Design by Sarah Fager, 2018

IKEA 365+ The 1990s began with a major recession, which brought an end to the 'more is more' mentality that dominated much of the Western world throughout the 1980s. In design, bold, postmodern playfulness gave way to a more practical minimalism.

For IKEA, this was an opportunity to refocus the company's efforts on their long-standing goal: to provide many people with functional, well-crafted products at low prices. In 1995, designers Susan Pryke, Anki Spets and Magnus Lindström were brought onboard to create a new kitchenware range, representing 'good everyday items'.

They made over seventy pieces, contrived to make cooking, serving and eating food both easier and more enjoyable. The use of long-lasting materials meant that the collection could be used daily, all year round – resulting in its name: IKEA 365+ (the 'plus' indicating that the products go that little bit further than expected).

Released in 1997, the IKEA 365+ range was an instant bestseller. The most recent collection, by Wiebke Braasch, Nike Karlsson, Henrik Preutz and Ola Wihlborg, launched in 2017, with the aim of helping customers to distil their kitchenware down to the essentials, and an increased focus on sustainability.

One of the most innovative offerings in this respect is the Good Design-awarded series of storage containers, which centre on reducing food waste. The containers are transparent, allowing customers to easily see leftovers in the fridge, and come with a selection of airtight lids for different uses. Meanwhile, the durable materials they're made from – borosilicate glass and polypropylene – can withstand rapid temperature changes, for swift transference from the freezer to the microwave.

HUVUDROLL Reducing our collective impact on the planet means making individual changes to our daily lives. One of the simplest things we can do is to eat more consciously, but all too often the most sustainable food options are also the most expensive.

That's not the case with IKEA's plant ball HUVUD-ROLL, the eco-friendly alternative to the company's iconic meatball, which arrived in IKEA restaurants in 2020, twenty-five years after its predecessor.

Keen to cater to plant-based customers, IKEA added vegetable balls to their menu in 2015, but the creation of the plant ball marked a more ambitious goal: to tempt all IKEA diners, including the meat eaters, into opting for the more conscious choice.

IKEA sells one billion meatballs per year, and the plant ball's climate footprint is just four per cent of that of the classic meatball, so even prompting the occasional switch from meat to plant ball on an individual scale could make a considerable difference.

To achieve this, however, the team knew they'd have to deliver a meatball equivalent that would satisfy even the greatest gourmands, while retaining the low price tag of the original meatball.

A long process of trial and error ensued, but eventually they came up with the ideal combination: yellow pea protein, oats, potato, onion, apple and seasoning. The plant ball is the healthier option too, making the transition all the more meaningful for our bodies, and our planet.

Design by IKEA of Sweden, 2020

RON

FINLEY

THE GARDEN OUTSIDE Ron Finley's home in South Central Los Angeles is a feast for the senses. Bright orange dragonflies, known as 'flame skimmers', dart through lush green foliage. Running water gurgles over smooth stones in what was once the deep end of an Olympic-sized swimming pool. Scents of citrus and lavender fill the air. If you listen closely, says Finley, you might hear the plants humming. 'I've had people come here and amplify the sounds these plants are giving off,' he says, sitting in the shade at his workbench in the heart of his garden. 'It's crazy! When they turned it up, you'd think you were listening to Phil Spector's *Wall of Sound*.'

Back in 2010, Finley decided to start making use of the often-neglected patches of dirt that run alongside roads in his neighbourhood. He planted vegetables, but was soon cited for 'gardening without a permit' by the City of Los Angeles. That sparked a horticultural revolution, as Finley and fellow green activists demanded – and won – the right to garden and grow food on their streets. He wasn't just making a point about urban land use, but also about access to fresh produce. South Central Los Angeles is a 'food desert', an area where access to healthy food options are extremely limited or non-existent. Now, through his garden and charity The Ron Finley Project, he is teaching his community how to grow fruit and vegetables for themselves – and advocating for social change.

KP: **When did you first realize you had green fingers?**

RF: When I was a young, young kid. This was one of my first hustles. We used to mow neighbours' lawns, pulling weeds and using the push mower. That's how we got money to go to the movie theatre.

KP: **You're a fashion designer by trade. Are there overlaps with gardening?**

RF: Of course. Where does fabric come from? Where do colours come from? It's all the same thing.

KP: **When you started planting vegetables along the streets of South Central in 2010, did you expect it to be so contentious?**

RF: Yeah, because I actually started way before that. The first time I did it I got a warrant for my arrest and had to go to court. I had to take everything out. When I did it the second time, in 2010, it was all going cool until a neighbour complained. If I saw that old lady again I would kiss her and buy her dinner. She was trying to get me into trouble, but when she complained

Words KEVIN E.G. PERRY
Photography MO MFINANGA

she started a chain of events. We got the law changed; I wound up talking all over the world. Now I tell people, 'Embrace your haters, because they will make you famous.'

KP: What is The Ron Finley Project?

RF: The Ron Finley Project is basically a think tank for what's possible. We want to change people's perception of what has value. People don't value themselves. We don't value soil. We don't value water, because we just turn on the faucet. The biggest thing we don't value is air, because we don't see it! But try doing without it and see what happens to you. We also show people how to garden. I'm trying to plant seeds in your mind and let you harvest the fruit that grows.

KP: What does it mean to have 23.5 million people in the US living in food deserts?

RF: I call them 'food prisons'. Deserts can be beautiful. Prisons not so much. These are neighbourhoods where there's no access to healthy food whatsoever. Why? If the powers that be wanted it there, it would be there. I was at a Mayor's conference and asked, 'Why are underserved neighbourhoods underserved?' 'Oh, you know, that's a big question.' I said, 'No, it's not. Underserved neighbourhoods are underserved 'cause you don't serve them.' It's that simple. In some

neighbourhoods, you say 'avocado toast' and it magically appears in your hands; in other neighbourhoods, dust appears. That shit's by design. If you want to fix something, you fix it. If you choose not to, it's because the people in these areas mean nothing to you.

KP: So what's the solution? Should we all be growing our own food?

RF: We all should be growing some of our food. Everybody on this planet should know how to grow food. It's not always necessary if you've got healthy food around, but if you don't, then you should know how to grow your food. It's a life skill, not a hobby.

KP: What if people don't have much outdoor space?

RF: When I talk to kids at colleges I tell them, 'You've got a balcony, you can get some food growing out there.' You get some salad and you make a meal for your boyfriend and girlfriend from your own garden. Grow some food and cook it. That shit is sexy.

KP: How does being out here in your garden make you feel?

RF: I feel like I've got a junkyard! I do understand what other people see when they come, even if it's not totally my vision yet. I've had people come here and cry. But

I don't want this to be special. I want people to be like, 'Your tomatoes ain't shit, look at mine!'

KP: Do you think this garden can inspire more like it around the city?

RF: Over time, it will. It will happen just like it happened here. When you think about it, beauty doesn't cost any more than ugly does. All it's about is the intent.

KP: What's your favourite thing to eat that you grow here?

RF: Mangoes! But we have everything. Gooseberries, blood oranges, sugar cane.

KP: What advice would you give people who'd like to start their own garden?

RF: Compost, compost, compost. Compost puts stuff back where it's supposed to be. I tell people, 'Be the forest.' When a tree falls in the forest, what happens to it? It becomes a habitat. Then it breaks down and goes back into the forest. No one's tilling soil. No one's spraying pesticide. That shit takes care of itself. The only thing that destroys forests are humans. That's why I say we need to change what we value. What are we going to do without Mother Nature? If you don't value your mother, you don't value yourself.

KP: Do you play music to the plants?

RF: Yeah, I play them house music. Soulful house and Afro house, and some Frank Sinatra, and some James Brown.

KP: What do they like the most?

RF: To be watered!

'I'm trying to plant seeds in your mind and let you harvest the fruit that grows.'

— RON FINLEY

Ritual:
Ron Finley prunes his herb garden

RON FINLEY starts each day the same way. 'I wake up, I sit up, I look up, I stand up, and I typically don't get caught up,' he says with a smile. 'That's my ritual. I look up and look in to give thanks for the fact that I've got another day to do this.' He says he lives his life firmly rooted in the present moment. 'People ask me about the future and I say, "What? Two minutes from now?"' says Finley with an incredulous note in his voice. 'What future are you talking about? If we don't fix this planet, there is no future.'

His daily routine in his verdant South Central garden varies depending on the seasons, but typically he'll set aside some time each day to go around with his trusty pruning shears, tending to the plants that need it. 'We deadhead a lot of the plants,' he explains, referring to the gardening practice of removing spent flowers to encourage the plants to grow back stronger. 'With a lot of the plants, once you trim them back they come right back, and some things if you don't trim them then they don't come back.'

He pays particular attention to his herb garden, where plants like lavender and basil can have their life cycles prolonged by careful pruning. 'You can get a big old bush that way because you're training it,' he says. 'The plant thinks: "Okay, I'm producing seed now," and you're like: "No, you're not!" It makes the plant get stronger and stronger, and bigger and bigger.'

When giving lessons to the budding gardeners who pay him a visit, Finley likes to remind them that most plants are hardier and more difficult to kill than many novices think. 'I mean, plants don't really want to die,' says Finley. 'They're literally alive.'

Words KEVIN E.G. PERRY
Photography MO MFINANGA

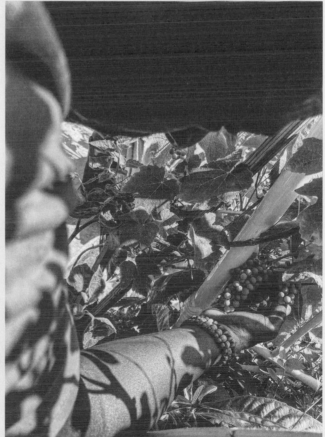

Photo Essay: Matthew Donaldson

'DON'T PLAY WITH YOUR FOOD!' It's a refrain that soundtracks mealtimes at dining tables around the world – but not Matthew Donaldson's. The photographer embraces play, mess and silliness, experimenting with his subjects – a humble banana or a half-dozen eggs – until he finds the 'oops' moment and the magic within it. Scrambled up in this approach, you'll find a pleasing appreciation of colour, texture and form. And you might never look at your dinner in quite the same way again.

KAMAL MOUZAWAK

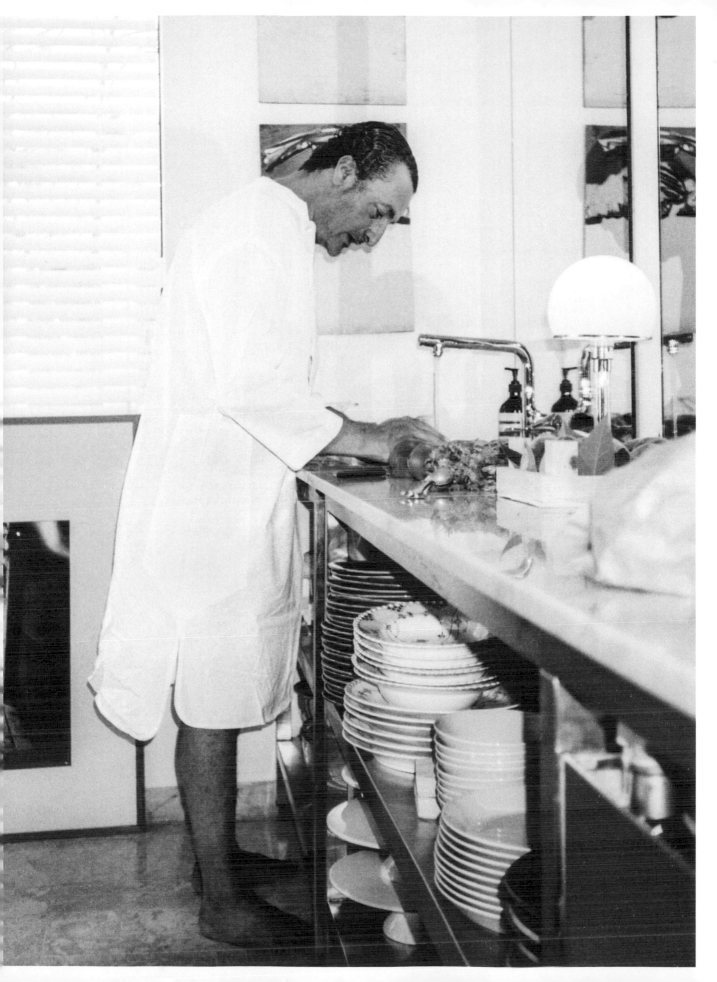

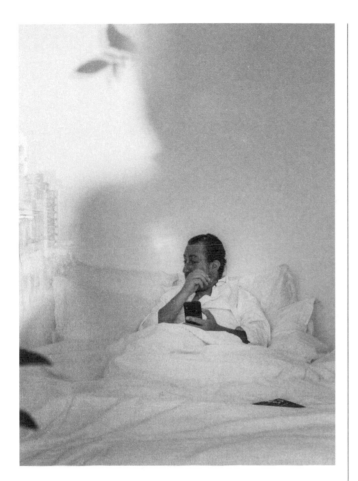

JUST AS ALL ROADS lead to Rome, any examination of Lebanese food culture leads to Kamal Mouzawak. It may come as a surprise to learn that a port city like Beirut, which once boasted a plethora of souks and bazaars, didn't have a produce market after its Civil War until Kamal founded Souk El Tayeb.

The souk started as an open-air weekly market for farmers and producers, and paved the way for Tawlet, a project for some of Lebanon's best cooks – home cooks – to make one of the most elaborate cuisines in the world accessible, preserving local culinary traditions. In the process, these projects empowered the cooks, most of them women, to become foundational contributors to the livelihood of their households.

These canteens expanded beyond the city itself, and soon Tawlet was popping up all over the country, celebrating regional cuisine and expanding the supply chain that came with them. Kamal's eco-touristic vision came full circle with the Beits – bed and breakfasts he opened across the country – executed with the same level of dedication, finesse and artistic simplicity as all of Souk El Tayeb's projects.

The first time I visited Kamal in his home was in 2012. It must have been summer, as I recall him making lemonade from scratch, skin in, the old Batrouni way. Ever since, I've been able to identify the Kamal Mouzawak touch in any space or act of hospitality from miles away.

JG: You've always lived between places. When people ask you where you live, what do you tell them?

KM: I'm living where I'm living in that second. People like you and me, who live between places, are always confronted with the questions 'Did you leave Beirut? Have you settled?' Settling in one place means you left the other one. For me, settling is not important. What's important is to have a safe space – a space I can go to and feel nurtured and protected, and bring others with me. And we have to ask ourselves, 'What have I contributed to this space?'

JG: You've been especially active in France lately.

KM: I am still trying to do the same thing, to promote Lebanon's traditions, its cuisine and its people. Tawlet Paris will follow the same model as Tawlet Beirut, with a Dekkene – a grocery store of the best products that represent Lebanon. Organic burghul, goat, cow and sheep labneh from the best animals in France, working with the best cheesemongers in Paris, La Fromagerie de Paris. This is the real embassy of Lebanon.

Words JADE GEORGE
Photography MOHAMAD ABDOUNI

FOOD

JG: How did your work in Lebanon change after the explosion on 4 August 2020?

KM: Lebanon is an extreme case of change ... the explosion, COVID, economic and political catastrophes. But change happens every day all around the world. Everyone has to acknowledge change, accept it and act accordingly. Practically, this meant closing all of our outlets. We had to focus on emergencies.

We created Matbakh El Kell, a community kitchen that produced around 2,000 meals a day. We moved near to ground zero of the explosion and put everything under one roof, all our markets, offices, Tawlet, Dekkene and Matbakh El Kell. It's like one big family hugging each other, a safe gathering space. Safe spaces are missing in this country.

JG: You also moved apartments. Why do you always live a stone's throw away from work?

KM: Commuting is one of those things I find horrendous. How can you lose so much time, energy, fossil fuel. I hate waste in general. When I have a project I try to live above it. I live in the building facing the new space. For me it's escaping to the middle of nowhere or zero commuting. Lately that's been Beit Douma or this apartment. I love this apartment.

JG: Like any property around the port, it bore a great deal of destruction. Tell me about its restoration.

KM: The apartment is about 80 square metres (861 square feet). You walk in and you're faced with a 4-metre (13-foot) wall, which I turned into a bookshelf, made with very thin steel and Bondi wood. When the city's reconstruction began, contractors were gathering things that they could give away, and they sent us these thick wooden panels they use in scaffolding on construction sites.

Behind my library is my bedroom. It is empty. It is all white. I have my bed. I have a Charlotte Perriand lounge chair in its original form. I have two huge plants, a philodendron and a colocasia. And then I have that view of the sea. When you walk in, your sight goes straight to the outside.

There's nothing on the walls but one image, by Franck Christen, which he shot in 2004 in Horsh Beirut. It was the first day of what later became Souk El Tayeb. So, it's very symbolic for me.

JG: I remember this kitchen from your previous apartments.

KM: Yes. It fits perfectly! I like the idea of 'I'll move and take things with me.' I don't have cupboards stuck to the wall, but rather elements that can be stored away to adapt to my needs.

JG: What is your relationship with design?

KM: As a young kid, I was a consumer of design and fashion. I thought I needed things to exist, but I understood with age that I exist by myself. I surround myself with objects that are needed. I'm a big worshiper of Bauhaus, and Bauhaus is about functionality. Objects have to be functional, durable and beautiful. For me, this is design.

JG: Where does your interest in food come from?

KM: My uncles and grandfather from my father's side were all farmers. My maternal grandfather was a shoemaker who owned agricultural land. As children, every October we went with him to pick apples. The women of the family expressed their care and love, and competed through cooking. I have always been sensitive to this.

Food is the most sincere expression of who we are. If you draw a map of just kibbe in Lebanon, you can draw the country's history of religion, geography and botany. Look at the kibbe nayye from Zgharta, with nothing in it but white pepper, and the kibbe from the South of Lebanon, with a whole garden foraged inside it. Look at the people. In the North, where there are rocky mountains, they're tough, and in the South, where there are soft hills, they are soft and sweet. Food is an important common ground to build on. It breaks boundaries and misconceptions.

JG: What do you like to do in your free time?

KM: I like to do nothing. I love my siestas. I read. I don't need to be active all the time, and I don't do lists anymore.

JG: What do you always pack?

KM: My phone [chuckles]. I travel light, with cabin luggage only. We clutter our lives with things; this is why our emotions get cluttered. I am not Zen, no. But I try to declutter as much as possible. When I visit friends I declutter their kitchen countertops.

JG: Do you take objects with you, for familiarity?

KM: Not at all. A new space is a blank canvas. Enjoy it, don't be afraid. Whatever it is we're doing, we have to do it fully. This is our contribution to life. I live by this.

'Food is an important common ground to build on. It breaks boundaries and misconceptions.'

— KAMAL MOUZAWAK

REST

REST IS VITAL both to our individual health, and to the health of the planet. In a contemporary society that demands we are always on – whether we're subject to high-pressure work schedules, meeting the needs of loved ones or hunched over our devices absorbing a never-ending onslaught of information – creating space for relaxation and restoration has become a revolutionary act.

Recent studies have found that there are no fewer than seven different types of rest, ranging from the physical and the mental to the creative and the emotional. Just as our homes are places of activity – preparing food, playing together, working or washing – they should be places of refuge too. A hideout from sensory stimulation and the rigour of everyday life outside. Perhaps that means somewhere that you can lean back and listen to music, or slip into a flow state, paintbrush in hand. Perhaps it's just about enjoying the company of friends.

In this chapter, our Icons approach this idea from three very different places. We look again at a simply designed rocking chair that recreates one of our most intuitive calming movements using renewable materials and artisanal craftsmanship. We consider a technological innovation that combines the soothing effects of light and sound in one, inspired by the quiet wonder of a roaring open fire. And we recall the minimal, modernist design signatures that allowed IKEA to reconnect with its Scandinavian roots in the 1990s, via that archetype of inactivity: the bed.

Rest for an athlete is a whole other story. New York-based artist, designer and skateboarder Alexis Sablone confesses that she doesn't find it easy. Her passion for skating, once a simple hobby, took her all the way to the Tokyo Olympics, and art and design have long been a means of making a living. She shares the thoughts that drift into her head while she's in child's pose, from the happy chaos of her Brooklyn home, in one of our Life Visits in this chapter.

For the Rodriguez-Martin Family, rest is interwoven with the way we use the Earth's resources. We visited their beautiful, calm home in Guadalajara, Mexico, to find out how innovative eco-technologies from solar panels to water filters combine with age-old materials such as adobe mud bricks, compost and sawdust, to create a home that is as gentle on the landscape as it is on the eye.

Finally, artist and photographer Brigitte Niedermair rests her eyes – as we all do – with a glance outside. The window of her studio in Merano, Italy, frames an ever-changing view of the forest landscape beyond it. As the days pass and the seasons change, she captures that sight in captivating detail. The resulting series, from which we share a small selection, is a poetic, restorative homage to the 1826 work, *View from the Window at Le Gras*, by French inventor Joseph Nicéphore Niépce – the oldest surviving photograph made using a camera.

IKEA PS GULLHOLMEN

SYMFONISK

BJÖRKVALLA

Design by Maria Vinka, 2002

IKEA PS GULLHOLMEN Some designs are inherently calming. Indeed, studies have found that the pendulous motion of a rocking chair releases endorphins in the brain that can improve mood, reduce stress and lessen pain. For Maria Vinka, the designer behind IKEA's petite but pioneering rocking chair IKEA PS GULLHOLMEN, it also offered a solution to her own innate restlessness.

The IKEA PS GULLHOLMEN was launched as part of IKEA's third PS collection, unveiled in 2002 and themed around pieces that could function both indoors and out. Keen to produce a design that would cater to those unable to sit still, and which would fit within her small one-bedroom apartment, Maria's response to the brief was a modern rocking chair made to occupy as little space as possible.

To achieve this, the designer reduced the chair to its essential parts – a gently curving seat and a miraculously slender backrest inspired by the handle of a *kåsa* (a traditional drinking cup – used by the Sámi, an indigenous Finno-Ugric people – with a hole in its curved stem for attachment to a belt).

The chair is created from woven banana fibre, a revolutionary choice of material at the time. Maria had come across the natural, biodegradable fibre, made from the stem of the banana tree, during an earlier trip to Vietnam. Formerly, these durable stems had been burned each time a tree's fruit was harvested, rendering the material a sustainable and low-cost option.

Moreover, when handwoven, the fibre, with its varying shades of creamy brown, boasts a pleasing wicker-like texture. For Maria, this proved the perfect means of imbuing her design with a sense of rural tranquility, as peaceful to look at as to sway on.

Design by Andreas Fredriksson and Iina Vuorivirta, 2019

SYMFONISK When it comes to creating a more restful environment at home, many rely on two key factors: light and sound. But both lamps and speakers take up space and add to the already vast tangle of electrical cords cluttering up modern homes.

With this in mind, IKEA paired up with wireless sound technology pioneers Sonos to devise the SYM-FONISK table lamp, made with an in-built Wi-Fi speaker. Just as a fireplace emits a warm light and calming crackle, the two teams sought to make a single product that offered the combined effects of soothing light and sound.

Designers Andreas Fredriksson and Iina Vuorivirta gave the lamp an organic form: a mouth-blown, opaque glass shade on a slimmer, but similarly curvaceous base containing the speaker. A woven textile cover in black or white discreetly functions as the speaker cloth, while the matching, round plinth on which the lamp sits adds to its sculptural effect.

Part of IKEA's and Sonos's ongoing partnership, centred around the democratization of great sound within the context of home furnishing, the speaker is designed to connect with any other Sonos product to enable stereo sound. This includes the two other members of the SYMFONISK family: the equally deft and duplicitous bookshelf and picture frame speakers.

Design by Ehlén Johansson, 1994

BJÖRKVALLA After the experimental design trends of the 1980s, a period of minimalism took hold, presenting a chance for IKEA to reconnect with its Swedish heritage as the 1990s progressed.

At the start of the decade, designer and long-time IKEA collaborator Ehlén Johansson was approached to create a series of high-end but still affordable bedroom furniture for IKEA, focused on 'modern Scandinavian design'.

Disenchanted with the stained beech and natural pine that dominated the range at the time, she put forward the idea for a collection in blond birch. A pale golden wood with strong Scandinavian roots, it was deemed an ideal fit for the concept.

The result was BJÖRKVALLA, which launched in 1994, a bedroom series defined by its practical functionality, elegant simplicity and calming natural warmth. These qualities lent the collection – which included beds, a side table and a chest of drawers – a wholesomeness and straightforwardness typical of traditional Swedish design, while the furniture's form was decidedly contemporary.

The most popular BJÖRKVALLA piece was the double bed, with its birch frame and gently tapered legs. The bed's most unique aspect was its adjustable rectangular headboard, made from woven ribbons of natural, unbleached cotton on a wooden mount. This could be positioned at different degrees from vertical to horizontal, for greater comfort when reading, resting or sleeping.

ALEXIS

SABOLNE

WHEN MOST PEOPLE hear the name Alexis Sablone, they might think of a professional skateboarder who represented Team USA at the 2020 Tokyo Olympics. Her fellow skaters might think of a pioneer for women's skateboarding, whose part in P.J. Ladd's 2002 video *Wonderful, Horrible, Life* is unmatched. Art aficionados might think of a phenomenal visual artist and architect. Alexis's existence proves that people can be complex and multidimensional, and excel in a variety of things. Not only has she earned a master's degree from MIT – exemplary for any normal person, let alone one of the world's best skaters – she's also designed shoes with Converse, and a skateable sculpture in Malmö, Sweden.

We met in her art studio in industrial Brooklyn to chat about her creative process. The room, which is brightly lit and satisfyingly messy, is full of sketches and unfinished sculptures. It also utilizes miscellaneous objects for unexpected uses: such as large cinder blocks for seating. The same is true in skateboarding, where a set of stairs might double up as an ideal skate spot. As both a skater and an architect, it's Alexis's ability to find multiple uses for an object that marries her two loves so harmoniously – and opens doors to a more sustainable world in the process.

BH: **How do art, architecture and skateboarding intersect in your life?**

AS: The way skateboarders, designers and architects see the space around them is very detailed. The types of things that they notice are similar, and they aren't things that other people take note of. Skateboarders are always looking for an opportunity to use the space around them creatively, in a way it wasn't designed to be used. Objects are usually so prescribed for regular people – benches for sitting, stairs for moving up and down, paths for walking on.

I think skateboarders are good at reducing the forms around them to obstacles that they can use in a totally different way. In that process, which happens naturally for a skateboarder, there's a connection to the way a designer looks at an existing space, or blank space, and tries to imagine something new. That process to me, as a skater and designer, feels similar. The iterative nature of design and the iterative nature of practising skateboarding – this kind of obsessive quality – ties it together.

BH: **Skateboarding has played into your perspective on public space, so much that you designed *Lady in the Square*, a skateable sculpture for a public square in Malmö, Sweden. How does that project reflect your vision?**

Words BRIANNA HOLT
Photography ARI MARCOPOULOS

AS: Malmö is a really unique place. Although it's a relatively small city, there is such a vibrant skate scene. The city seems to be pretty open-minded and sees an opportunity in the way skateboarders use and value the space around them, in a way that most populations don't.

Approaching something from the design side, with skateboarding in mind, creates a third condition – one where it's not built one way and misused by skaters, or built another way, then transformed to become an opportunity. Instead it's interesting for skaters, but also not immediately able to be read by non-skateboarders. That space for interpretation also creates a space for play and imagination – it becomes something you can sit or climb on.

BH: **You have officially made the US Olympic team for the Tokyo 2020 Olympics, the first time in history that skateboarding has been included. What are you most excited about?**

AS: The Olympics are so foreign to skateboarding, and vice versa, and to be a part of the first of anything is exciting. I'm curious to see the other athletes who are the best at what they do, who have trained for this and looked forward to it their whole lives. No part of me started skateboarding because I dreamed of being an Olympian. I just see it as an honour.

The optimistic part of me hopes that it will bring a good, new kind of attention to skateboarding, and with it respect from the outside. I hope people will look at skaters on the street and suddenly see that this is a determined and dedicated person, who is working on something – not someone dragging around a piece of wood.

BH: **How does sustainability and living more responsibly play into the skateboarding world?**

AS: Skateboarding builds a community really fast. You can meet another skateboarder and really become friends in a number of hours, because you have this thing in common that you both care about. It can powerfully build a physical community, aside from it just being something that you can do outside, and I think

that's an increasingly important quality when it comes to living more responsibly. The community and the friendships I've made through skateboarding have lasted me most of my life.

It also pushes you to focus. There's this kind of structure to skateboarding – as ruleless and as open as it is – because you can't skip steps and learn a certain kind of trick before you've built foundational skills. It's not instant gratification in any way. The work and time you put in changes you, in a good way. You grow from it. The experience of failure and repetition allows you to connect so quickly with other skateboarders, because only they understand what it takes, what you go through. It's a very powerful culture.

'Skateboarders are always looking for an opportunity to use the space around them creatively, in a way it wasn't designed to be used.'

— ALEXIS SABLONE

BH: **How do you really rest both body and mind?**

AS: It's really hard for me to turn my mind off, or stop thinking about either a project or skating. Even when I go to a yoga class and I'm supposed to be focusing on breathing I'm like, 'ooh, I'm in child's pose, I can think about my projects.' Reading and watching films, being immersed in a different story, helps me to relax, and not think so much about my own.

I got sick with COVID at the very beginning of the pandemic, before lockdown, and I had a fever and was so cold, so I started taking baths. Now that I live with my girlfriend and am not sharing a bathroom with a few different roommates, I don't mind soaking in the tub. So, now in the winter, I'll take a warm bath every day and put an audiobook on to relax.

Ritual:
Alexis Sablone makes coffee every morning

ALEXIS SABLONE, like many other New Yorkers, starts her mornings with coffee – and she makes it herself. Her set-up is simple: she uses a percolator, a red tea-pot for hot water, and half-and-half for added flavour. As for the grounds, Alexis and her girlfriend splurged on a coffee subscription at the height of the pandemic, and have no plans to cancel their membership anytime soon. 'It's kinda fun,' she says. 'They send you a different coffee every month, so I'm always trying something new.'

Despite the simplicity of her routine, Alexis does have some requirements: she drinks it hot, not iced, and out of her favorite mug. 'I'm pretty stubborn about coffee. I don't like drinking cold coffee, even when it's 100 degrees outside,' she says. She uses a mug made especially for her by her girlfriend, who is a full-time ceramist. 'If I use a regular-sized mug, then I won't even finish half of my coffee, and it drives my girlfriend crazy. So, she made me a smaller version of one of the regular-sized mugs she makes.'

As a routine coffee drinker, Alexis can't miss a morning, but it isn't because she'll feel lousy throughout the day or struggle with staying awake. 'It helps get me out of bed, but I don't know how much of that has to do with the actual caffeine, and how much of it is just because it's a taste that I look forward to,' she says. During graduate school, Alexis claims she built a tolerance for caffeine, so much that she could drink an espresso right before bed and have no trouble falling asleep. 'I really just like the ritual aspect of it. It's one of the few constants of my day.'

Words BRIANNA HOLT
Photography ARI MARCOPOULOS

Photo Essay: Brigitte Niedermair

THERE'S SOMETHING DEEPLY calming about routine. From the window of her studio in Merano, Italy, Brigitte Niedermair looks out on an ever-changing forest landscape – a sight that is at once profoundly restorative and vividly alive. Using just her phone – a respite from the 4x5-inch camera employed for the rest of her work – the artist captures this change on a regular basis, documenting both the world outside and her own shifting interior life. It's a fitting homage to French inventor Joseph Nicéphore Niépce's 1826 work, *View from the Window at Le Gras*. For Brigitte, nature serves as both a tonic and a tribute.

THE RODRIGUEZ-MARTIN FAMILY

MADE PRIMARILY OF adobe mud bricks, clay, rammed earth and wood, the home of Gabriela Martin and Mauricio (Maiz) Rodriguez sits on a modest plot of land that was once part of a family farm on the north-western outskirts of Guadalajara in Mexico.

El Nido de Tierra, or 'The Earth Nest', as it is called, was built gradually over several years – first to house the couple, and later to accommodate their two young sons, seven-year-old Pablo and three-year-old Samuel. The home radiates a feeling of warmth and comfort, in part due to the generosity of its main, central space: an open living-dining area framed by large sliding glass doors, which gracefully dissolve the distinction between inside and outside.

But beyond its aesthetic charms are a series of subtle but powerful ecological technologies that help the home maintain its light footprint. Composting systems create fertilizer from food scraps, as well as from the family's dry toilet. A solar panel heats water, which, once used, is naturally filtered through underground chambers to irrigate the garden.

The couple met at university, where they were both avid cyclists involved in local environmental groups. As an architecture student, Maiz spent a formative year living with a Wixárika community in the arid northern Sierra of Jalisco, where Gabriela often visited him. It was an experience that influenced them both greatly. As they explain, this time helped reframe the way they live, which in turn led to the construction of their first small home.

EC: **What took you to the Sierra Wixárika?**

GM: Maiz went there to build a dry toilet in the village school, so people didn't have to waste water. That area is really, really dry; there's no food, no water, no nothing. People have to go and fill buckets of water just to have in their houses.

MR: Gaby used to visit me there, and we lived in very basic conditions. And that's when I began to think it was possible to live differently.

GM: But, we were boyfriend and girlfriend. We didn't have a house; we didn't have anything.

EC: **How did the opportunity to build your first home come about?**

GM: Maiz's family had a farm in Penjamillo, and his father gave a piece of it to us. So, we thought, let's do something there. I said, 'We should build a dry toilet!' My friends used to make fun of me, saying that

Words EMMA CAPPS
Photography PIA RIVEROLA

instead of an engagement ring, Maiz gave me a toilet, because it was the first thing we built together. And then after that, we also built a small one-room home to live in.

It's quite funny because we'd just gotten married, and we were swept away with our ideas about sustainability and being in love – so we went there with only our dry toilet, to live in this tiny room.

But it was difficult to find jobs in the town there. I was teaching English at the local high school, but there weren't a lot of clients around for Maiz. After a year, he got offered a job at an architecture firm in Guadalajara, so we moved.

EC: **It sounds like even as a young couple, your thoughts about sustainable living were very aligned.**

MR: It was always a thing between the two of us, that I would think something and tell her, and she would think something and tell me, and it would flow, and we would understand each other.

GM: It was amazing because we studied different things and had different backgrounds, but we were both convinced by the idea of living a different life. We were against the odds and what other people said, so it was really nice that we were always on the same page.

EC: **And how about this home? How did you approach the process of building it?**

GM: We always said we didn't want to take out a loan. So, when we had a bit of money, we built the first part, and then, over many years, built the rest. And because of Maiz's work as an architect, we had the chance to do it ourselves. In the beginning, we had [just a bathroom], one room to live in and a cooler for our food.

EC: **And you were building almost exclusively with natural materials, which I imagine your contractors weren't so familiar with using?**

MR: The interesting thing is that the [builders] will always say, 'This is not going to work.' But once they see

how noble the process is and realize they don't have to buy expensive materials, they say, 'Ah, I can build this way.' So, it breaks a paradigm for them.

EC: **Is the home complete now, or do you still have ambitions you'd like to fulfil?**

GM: One big thing we haven't completely figured out yet is that we really want to grow all of our own food, but we're lacking the skills and time. And, our roofs were built to capture rainwater, but we haven't managed to set that up yet. So, we still have things we haven't finished, and sometimes we get frustrated, but it's like – we're getting there, it's OK.

EC: **Why is living sustainably important to you?**

GM: We always wanted there to be a congruence between what we think and what we do. We couldn't be thinking that we wanted to take care of the planet and not doing it; it's just not us.

MR: And if we can do something, well, we're going to do it. It's not a radical posture.

GM: And then, with the kids, we thought it was super nice to teach them to live a different life, and to be more aware.

EC: **So, it's just a part of their lives from the very beginning.**

GM: Exactly. I remember the first time Pablo saw a regular toilet in my parents' house, he said, 'Mum, they literally throw clean water down the toilet.' For him, it was like, 'That's just a waste, why do they do that?'

EC: **Your approach seems remarkably pragmatic and optimistic.**

GM: We were always really concerned about climate change, but we didn't want to get stuck focusing on the bad things happening in the world. Instead, we wanted to ask ourselves what was possible. I mean, the ideal is one thing, but what is actually possible? We always thought, if it's up to us to do something, let's do it

'We didn't want to get stuck focusing on the bad things happening in the world. Instead, we wanted to ask ourselves what was possible.'

— GABRIELA MARTIN

PLAY

PLAY IS A powerful thing. We play music, sports, games, pretend. Through it, we connect, create, recharge, escape and explore. From play, ideas emerge; ideas turn into experiments; and with enough room for mistakes, experiments soon turn into innovations. Without which, of course, all hope of ever working towards a more sustainable future would be instantly quashed.

Today's young people will inherit a world vastly different to the one we were born into – one with its own 'wicked problems'. Our role now, beyond doing everything in our power to lessen our expenditure of the Earth's natural resources, is to equip the next generation with all the tools they might need. In large part, through play.

For IKEA, children have always been the most important people in the world. In the late 1990s, it introduced a new range of safe, secure children's toys, furniture and other wares rooted in in-depth research into children's development. A huge success, it was the springboard for two of this chapter's Icons: an inexpensive foldable gym mat that lends itself to practising somersaults or building forts; and a miniature kitchen, created by the designer behind the full-size version, complete with realistic sink, oven and microwave, and even a light-up hob. Finally, we tell the origin story behind a simple, sturdy sofa with a removable, easy-to-wash cover – difficult to destroy, and ideal for play.

Whatever your age, play is central to creativity. For Jean-Charles Leuvrey, that has always meant following his passion. He founded independent radio station Hotel Radio Paris in 2016 as a platform for musicians, DJs, producers and spoken word artists, to allow the city's independent music culture to flourish. But play also takes him into forests, up mountains and on treks through wild landscapes, reconnecting with the natural world in order to reconnect with himself. Most recently, it has meant a move to a barge just outside the French capital, where he can while away days catching fish. We visit him there.

An artist who favours bright colours, fluffy characters and big, bold ideas, Misaki Kawai's practice has long been synonymous with fun. But it would be nothing without the rigour of her daily life at home – wherever that may be – with her partner Justin and their five-year-old daughter Poko. Together, they learn, snack, make and play, bouncing off one another and having a jolly time in the process. Just one week after moving from Los Angeles, they invited us into their new home in Copenhagen, to get a glimpse of their life for ourselves.

Play is also the thread that winds its way through every vivid still-life scene Hugo Yu creates. For our Photo Essay this chapter, the New York-based artist scoured West Coast goodwill stores for pre-loved odds and ends to take apart and put back together, creating a series of structures inspired by the wave of nostalgia that hit him on seeing the sunset over a kids' park. Recycling, ingenuity and silliness combined, to charming effect.

PLUFSIG

DUKTIG

KLIPPAN

Design by Tina Christensen, 2014

PLUFSIG IKEA has long understood the importance of play to a child's physical, creative and social development. Ingvar Kamprad first introduced play areas into IKEA stores in the 1960s and, in 1997, launched Children's IKEA, a range aimed at facilitating learning through play.

Since 2010, IKEA has also conducted regular Play Reports, interviewing thousands of parents and children worldwide to understand how design can better serve the purpose of play at home.

The inaugural report revealed that many families were living in small urban homes, with limited access to outdoor play spaces. Parents were also worried that digital entertainment was distracting their children from getting enough physical exercise.

Looking to address both of these concerns, IKEA came up with PLUFSIG, an inexpensive foldable play mat, which arrived in stores in 2014. The multicoloured design was conceived by Tina Christensen in collaboration with Swedish contemporary circus company Cirkus Cirkör, who lent their acrobatic insight.

While initially intended as a soft surface for gymnastics, which stimulates children's sense of balance and coordination, PLUFSIG is surprisingly versatile. Children can lie on it to read, transform it into a fort, or pile multiple mats on top of one another to make a larger play area.

The design's PEVA cover (a non-chlorinated vinyl) and its lightweight polythene-foam filling make it easy to clean and carry, while its concertina-like panels allow it to be tucked away discreetly at the end of the day.

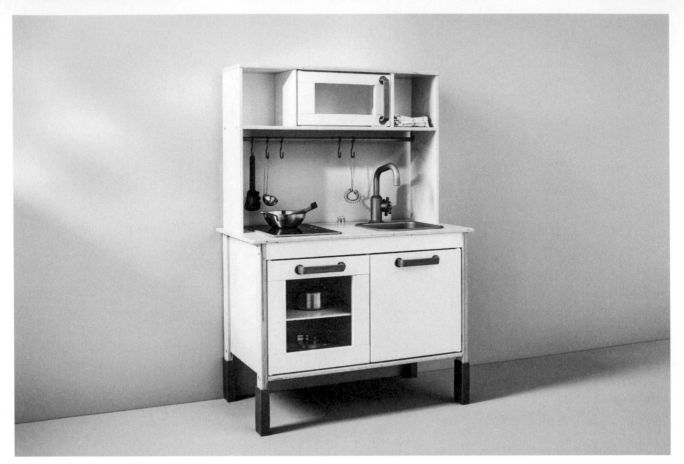

Design by Mikael Warnhammar, 2007

DUKTIG Role-play is vital for the development of a child's social skills. And when it comes to imitating adult life, the more authentic-looking the toys, the more realistic the play. Plus, a well-made playset tends to last longer, and look better.

In the early 2000s, aware that the market was oversaturated with cheap and childish toy designs made from blow-moulded plastic, IKEA had the idea of producing an attractive, high-quality kitchen playset based on one of its own adult kitchens.

The company's new VÄRDE kitchen unit, a blond birch design with a modern Scandinavian aesthetic, seemed like the ideal fit. Designer Mikael Warnhammar was enthused by the concept and set about creating a miniature mock-up of his kitchen, even inserting two decorative LED lamps from the existing IKEA range into the kitchen counter to emulate an electric hob.

The team was impressed and, after further development, the DUKTIG toy kitchen was released in 2007, comprising a realistic sink, oven and microwave, various storage spaces and, of course, the light-up hob.

The birch playset was designed with longevity in mind; it is made from safe, durable and recyclable materials, while its adjustable legs have three height settings, allowing it to grow alongside a child. Younger children can play with its accompanying accessories, from pots and pans to spatulas and coffee cups, while older children can use it to adopt the role of budding chef or lucrative restaurant owner, with a little help from the DUKTIG toy till.

KLIPPAN The 1970s saw much of the Western world embrace a more liberal attitude. Children were being raised with a stronger focus on play and self-expression, and while once their indoor pursuits may have been confined to a single area, there was now a greater need to play-proof the home.

In 1979, following the irreparable damage of an expensive Italian sofa at the hands of his young children, Lars Engman, former head of design and product developer at IKEA, realized the need for a new type of couch: one that could endure the impact of everyday play, without forgoing its aesthetic appeal.

The first thing that sprung to mind was IKEA's simple yet sturdy sofa LAPPMON, by Japanese designer Noboru Nakamura, which, with a few modifications, would meet all the criteria for a child-friendly couch.

To start, the redesign would need removable, easy-to-wash covers – a first for IKEA, which had previously offered dry-clean-only options. To achieve this, Lars reduced LAPPMON's measurements to match the standard width of fabric at the time and set out to find the minimum amount of material required to dress the couch, while fitting inside a household washing machine.

By 1980, KLIPPAN had launched a two-seater, wooden-framed love seat so compact that it could fit comfortably through most household doorways. Sales were slow at first, but customers soon cottoned on to KLIPPAN's many benefits. Not only was it ideal for family homes and small living spaces alike, its changeable covers meant that it could be endlessly updated according to changing interior design trends.

Over the years, IKEA has made small alterations to KLIPPAN's design to render it even more lightweight and affordable, including the decision to flatpack it in 2004. All of which has contributed to its ongoing status as an IKEA classic.

Design by IKEA of Sweden, 1980

JEAN-CHARLES

LEUVREY

CAN YOU GET seasick on a river? The answer is 'absolutely not,' according to Jean-Charles Leuvrey, Hotel Radio Paris founder and jack-of-all-trades, who recently moved with his wife to a barge just outside of Paris, in the adjacent city of Bezons. Until then, the couple lived in the centre of the capital. They decided to look for a long-term solution that would bring them closer to nature, and allow them easy access to fishing, all while remaining in close proximity to the Hotel Radio Paris studio, in the 18th *arrondissement*.

Jean-Charles founded the radio station in 2016, and has been maintaining its independence and total freedom ever since. Hotel Radio Paris is a platform for anybody who passionately wants to try something out – be it live music, mixing or spoken word. In that respect, it's a space dedicated to play; playing music, playing around, playing with different ideas and forms of expression. Often before they know it, those who are discovered by Jean-Charles become huge sensations. Because Jean-Charles, whose journey took him from working as a trader in London, to skating intensely in South Africa and Barcelona, is also a trendsetter, happy to work in the shadows while doing consulting work for some of the most influential companies today. And for him, the shadows are the privacy of his boat.

HT: **How did you end up living on a boat?**

JCL: The story is quite funny actually. I am someone who has to do a lot of things, I am uber excited as a person. I had been in Paris for nearly six years. I've travelled a lot in my life, and I hate Paris, it's getting really annoying. Through my work I have always been in contact with creative people, so sometimes when you go back home you want to be disconnected from that shit. I grew up in Africa, in Tchad, I had a funny start to life. So, basically, I always had this need to do stuff outside. Last week I was in Chamonix and we spent two days at Mont Blanc, which was covered in snow. I go hiking and mountaineering as well. That's also the reason why I started skating when I was really young, and I still skate. I also like fishing. I love to be outdoors, but the fishing is the funniest part.

HT: **So, you needed a place where you could fish?**

JCL: Yes. I told my wife I wanted to buy land next to the river, somewhere outside of Paris, and build a tiny house. I know how to build shit. Because I used to build skateparks. Somewhere we could go every weekend and chill. But I didn't find the perfect place. Then I started seeing barges in my research. I was like, it looks funny. My wife suggested that we actually go and visit

Words HAYDÉE TOUITOU
Photography JULIEN T. HAMON

LIFE VISIT

one. We got hooked on the idea, and eventually we found this one.

HT: How long have you been living here?

JCL: We bought the place in December last year, and we refurbished everything – insulation, painting, changing the windows, etc. It took four months. So, we've been living here for a month and a half. It's brand new. I mean, I feel we live in a house to be honest. A house on the water. It looks like a boat, but if you blank out the water, it's just a really nice house. It's the best thing I've done in a while.

HT: What is your favorite spot on your boat?

JCL: I love our room, but my favourite spot might be around this table. I love looking out of this window and seeing what's around. But maybe it's too new, still, to know my favourite spot.

HT: What led you to create a radio station?

JCL: I created Hotel Radio Paris five years ago, in February 2016. I actually had a radio show when I was sixteen, with my next door neighbour, a guy called Brodinski, who then became one of the most famous DJs in the 2010s. We had a show together for two years. After my studies I was a trader in London, then I became freelance. We did so much stuff, I mean, I still do. But at some point, while working for some other radios here and there, I decided I could move to Paris and have a radio show where I would invite people on and interview them about how to live off your passion.

HT: What was your vision for Hotel Radio Paris?

JCL: I decided to create Hotel Radio Paris with one idea in mind: never segment anything. Have all the music together. As long as I dig your vibe and that your sound is cool, you're welcome. That's my main thing. Hotel Radio Paris, even before being a radio station, is an exploration platform. People can reach out and suggest

stuff to me. It is the launching pad for so many of the most successful people today.

HT: **Your work is your passion, and vice versa. How do you find time to play?**

JCL: Everything becomes a job. That's why I gave myself five more years before disappearing. It's impossible. My wife had to ask me how it is that even our hobbies have become a job. It's not my fault, people dig my vibe. And I also love doing that for people. Even hiking and mountaineering became a job! The wonderful thing is that it allows me to be always on vacation, and never on vacation at the same time. I'm absolutely off three weeks a year, and I go on treks. That's my way of escaping, even if it's hard. I create this isolation for three weeks, to be able to deal with the wave of people during the year ahead. But it is also exhausting, and that's why I chose to live here now. This is a place where I can chill, even if the phone rings all day long.

'The wonderful thing is that [my life] allows me to be always on vacation, and never on vacation at the same time.'

— JEAN-CHARLES LEUVREY

Ritual: Jean-Charles Leuvrey fishes from his boat

JEAN-CHARLES LEUVREY's primary motivation for moving into a barge located just outside of Paris was to have easy access to the water, in order to fish whenever he wanted to. 'Fishing is my yoga, for real,' he explains, arranging his rod so that the line drifts out from the back of the boat. 'It's ultra relaxing because a good part of it is detangling knots. And I love it.'

Before the boat was even an idea in both his and his wife's mind, they planned to stay in the centre of the city, but looked for land to be able to escape from time to time. And the peace that comes with life outside of the city – and specifically, from life on the water – was appealing.

He certainly knows his stuff. 'There are two kinds of fishing, in life,' he says. 'One is active fishing, and the other is more laid-back. So, I do both, but the laid-back kind is what I really enjoy. I sit on my chair. No one is talking to me, I'm not even checking my phone. It's the best.'

His goal is to catch each fish once, and then let it go without hurting it. 'I'm team no kill,' he says. 'Catch and release. I will never eat a fish that I caught. We have to save the fish! There are no more wild fish. If I eat one, it means that species might not be able to reproduce. So, I am very careful with what I fish.'

Nonetheless, he takes a rigorous approach to ticking off his list, sourcing the supply he needs for each catch. 'It's also super geeky, with the bait,' he adds. 'People who fish are real nerds. It's so cool, all these fake little fish. I'm really geeky with that. I buy some in Japan, and everything.'

Words HAYDÉE TOUITOU
Photography JULIEN T. HAMON

RITUAL

Photo Essay: Hugo Yu

HUGO YU was out running in California one evening when he stumbled across a kids' park. It was the feeling this sight evoked – one of pure nostalgia, recalling the ease, elation and total abandonment of childhood – that captured him. His resulting still-life sculptures are made using found and pre-loved objects: household gadgets, old toys and recycled knick-knacks, taken apart and then reassembled in new configurations. Because as any child will tell you, the best toys aren't toys at all.

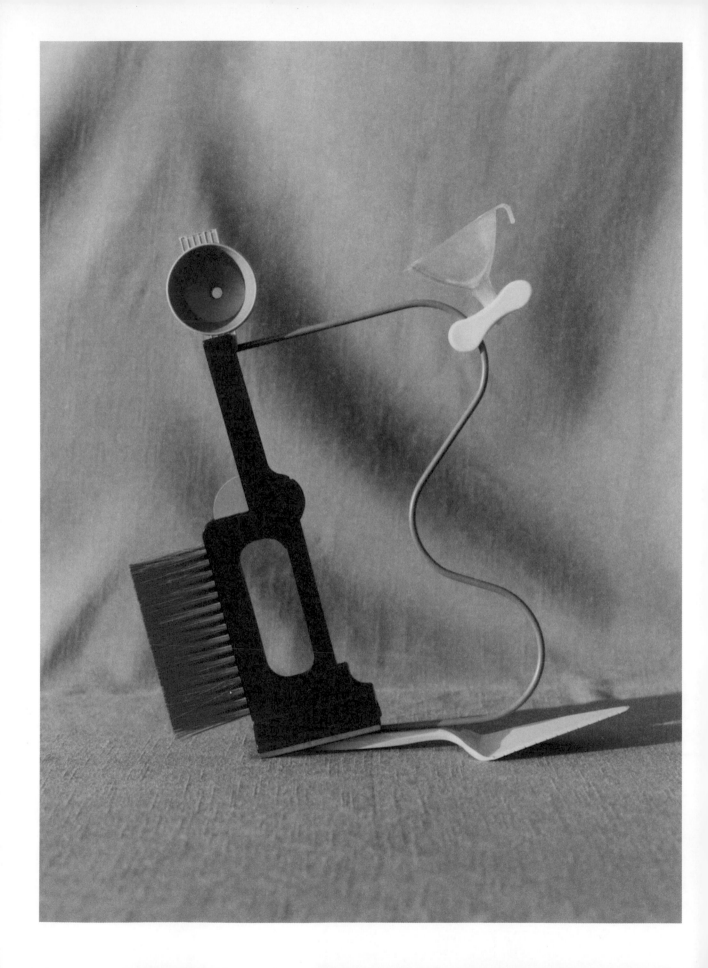

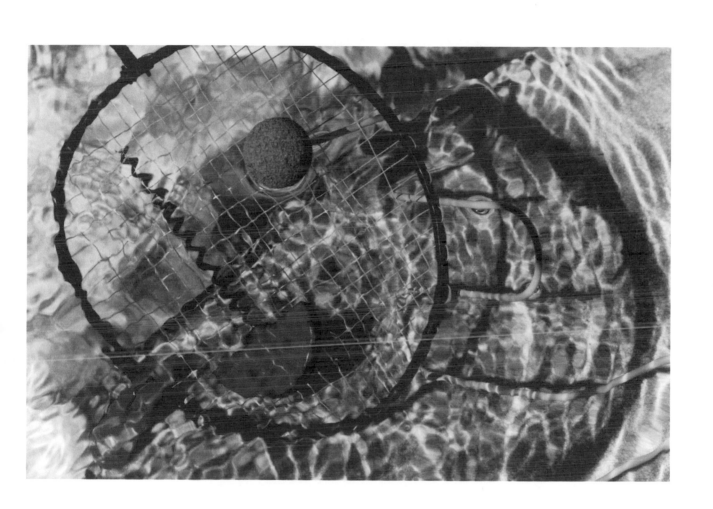

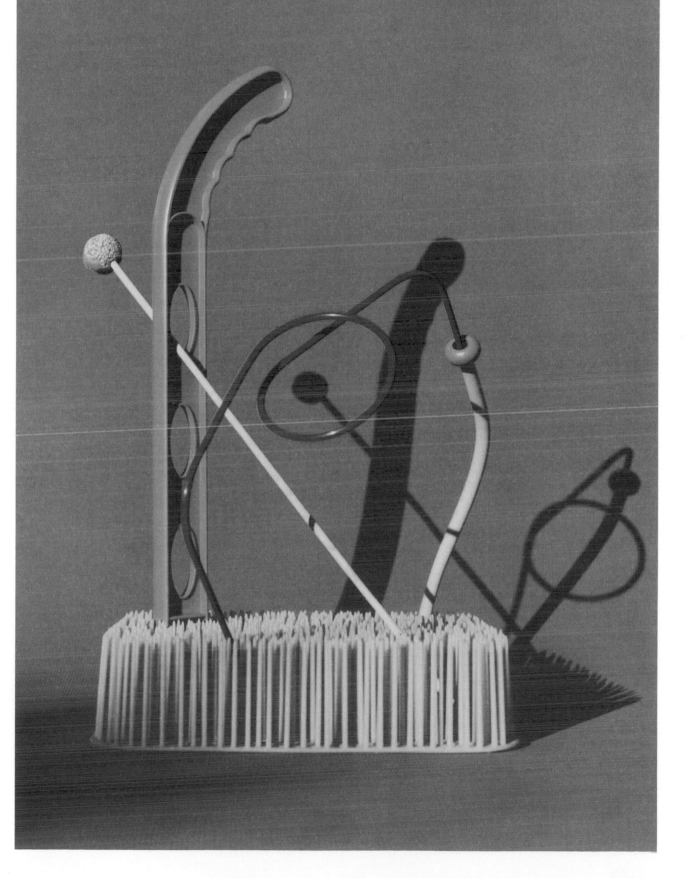

MISAKI

KAWAI

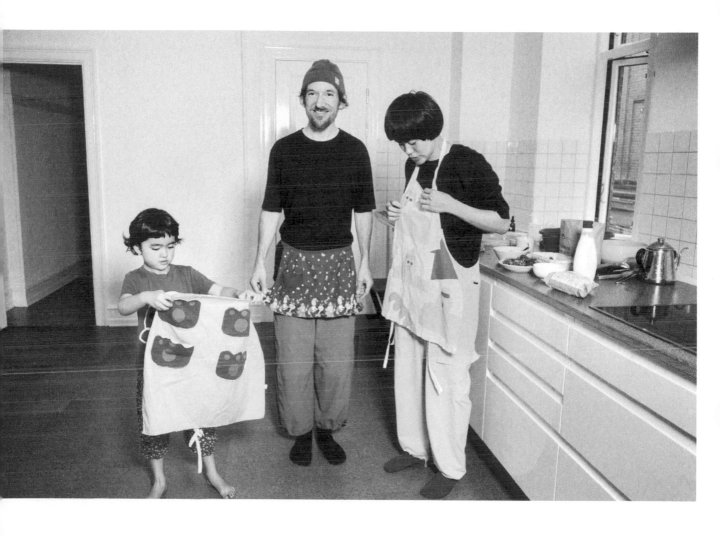

PLAY

ARTISTS MISAKI KAWAI, Justin Waldron and their five-year-old daughter Poko are currently residing in a flat in Copenhagen. They moved there just over a week ago, closely followed by one small crate of possessions shipped from their last home in Los Angeles.

Misaki's paintings and enormous fluffy creatures, on the other hand, are living in storage units and galleries all over the world, presumably whispering to one another about where Misaki, Justin and Poko might have gone. Her uninhibited, happy multimedia work, which depicts (among many things) snacks, humans, flowers, animals and smiles, is represented by galleries in New York, Japan and Copenhagen, to great acclaim. Everything she creates seems to exude joy, positivity and fantasy. It's occasionally referred to as 'childlike', which is not untrue, but is slightly reductive: this hard-working creative has the enviable talent of communicating her extraordinary imagination on canvas, in sculptural characters or in drawings, small publications and objects. Tying all of these media together is her sense of boundless, uninhibited freedom, and a gentle encouragement to the viewer to be more playful, curious and open.

The temporary apartment Misaki and her family now find themselves in has the unmistakable echo of a new and not-yet-furnished home, and is filled only with a handful of important items they chose to bring with them to start their new life. Misaki's new fabric tapestries are hung on the wall. Poko's art table is set up and covered in paints and paper. One of the high-ceilinged, bright, empty bedrooms is now a minimalist yoga studio (created by unrolling three yoga mats on the wooden floor – voilà!). They don't seem hugely bothered by furniture – where many people surround themselves with sofas, tables and small furnishings, these three just need paper and pens and somewhere to cook and eat rice together. Copenhagen might even be a temporary stop. The nomadic family are discussing potentially moving on to Taipei, a destination that appeals in terms of satisfying Misaki's craving for a more Asian way of life, but mostly for the food the city offers.

Here, Misaki has access to a studio in the city where she is able to make larger-scale works. It's empty at the moment, save for a hammock. The family spends most of their time in the apartment, which is a living space, a working creative studio and Poko's homeschool, all in one. Poko is a prolific zine-maker, the results of which are stacked together in the bookshelf. Any work the family makes goes straight on the wall. Poko, however, skips that step by drawing directly onto the windows.

They have an intrinsically creative life, with weekends following the same schedule as weekdays. At

Words LIV SIDDALL
Photography CASPER SEJERSEN

PLAY

7 a.m. the family wakes up. They eat breakfast at 8 a.m., while practising their Mandarin, and then they get to work on whatever they'd like to make that day. They might take a trip to the local playground on a Christiania bike, with Misaki and Poko sitting in the wagon in front. Whether it's Tai Chi, learning a new language or making a snack, they do it together.

LS: Do you dream of a permanent home?

JW: We do dream of permanence. We will build a home eventually, but where?

MK: Maybe somewhere green.

LS: What's the most important thing a home should have?

MK: I would say a city would be hard, of course, to build something in. So, it also could be minimal, but something playful and [a place that] anyone can just come and stay, and make something altogether. Maybe spend more time in nature, so everybody can be relaxed.

JW: Something we're always looking for in each space is to allow a nice workflow, because we have quite a structured routine every day. A space that allows Poko to create easily, that can accommodate our daily routine. Not too big of a kitchen, not too big of a space,

just right. By moving to all of these different places, we're researching, in a way.

MK: A kitchen is nice when it is small. You can grab things.

LS: A lot of creative people tend to do creative work in a studio, then go home just to sleep or eat. For you guys, it seems more fluid.

MK: It's hard for me to separate it. I don't feel like it's 'now this is my work time, time to go to the studio!' I just wake up, eat, maybe do yoga or something. Then I just do a little bit of painting, then go somewhere, then make a snack, make something, then maybe have a little party, just the three of us.

JW: It's quite efficient to just have the studio, or a workplace, in the home. Especially for Misaki. Unless the scale of the work becomes too big, then we need the studio space.

LS: When you move into an empty house, or an empty space, what's the first thing you do to make it feel like home?

MK: My grandma always told me, 'if you move, bring rice first, don't bring futon.' That's what she said. 'Bring rice, it's home. You're never going to starve, and if you bring futon, you'll just end up sleeping all the time in the bed.'

Or you know, I just make something, or Poko makes something or draws all over the window. It's just instant decoration, it feels homey.

JW: Rugs are a big one. These rugs are the ones we have lived with in Kyoto and LA. It's something you can just unroll and it's done. You could sleep on them too, if you didn't have a mattress.

LS: **What's the best thing about working as a family together?**

MK: Maybe [the way] we can play and work. We can always play, we can always work.

JW: One thing I've noticed is that Misaki and Poko bounce off each other a lot. Misaki is now working with a fashion label in Shanghai. She'll be designing, just sketching in a sketchbook, and Poko will be right there next to her, also sketching, kind of based on Misaki's sketches. Then Misaki is getting ideas in turn from Poko's drawings. It's a really amazing echo, if you will.

MK: She takes my idea and I take her idea, so we are working together. I'll be looking at what she's doing and thinking, 'hmm, maybe I can loosen up a little bit more.'

LS: **So, you all inspire each other?**

MK: I think so, yeah.

LS: **You seem to live together very harmoniously and happily.**

JW: We think so. We're very different in a lot of ways. Our visions are similar, but our roles are very different. We think that makes for a good team.

LS: **What makes a happy house?**

MK: I don't think it's much [to do with] objects. I feel it's more like feeling home, like coming home. You know, you can eat nice, warm food in the house, you can relax in the house. I think just making your own castle. It doesn't mean it's [an actual] castle, it just means it's a castle in the heart. A feeling.

'My grandma always told me, "if you move, bring rice first, don't bring futon."'

— MISAKI KAWAI

TOGETHERNESS

ACTION STARTS WITH the individual. But when it comes to the climate crisis, it's all too easy to get caught up in our singular, separate solutions and forget about the power of the people. A reusable coffee cup, a well-worn cotton tote bag and a pair of jeans made from recycled denim are all small, noble efforts, alone. Scaled up – think: one billion coffee cups, tote bags, pairs of jeans – they have a visible, tangible impact. It is up to each of us to do everything in our power to make small changes in our day-to-day lives, and to encourage those around us to make small changes in theirs too.

For IKEA, this means designing out waste. It means introducing buy-back schemes. And it means making sustainable options so affordable that they become the default choice for millions of users around the world. Small changes, made at scale, create big impacts.

Take for example the LED light bulb, examined in this chapter's Icons. Once relegated to the costly upper end of the price bracket, it made high-quality, low-energy lighting the reserve of the rich – until IKEA succeeded in manufacturing one for less than one euro, altering the market forever. Similarly, nine in ten of us breathe air that exceeds the World Health Organization's guideline limit for pollutants – and that's indoors as well as out. In the pages that follow, we consider a sleek but affordable air purifier designed to minimize this harm at home. Finally, big things occasionally come in very small packages. Such as the water nozzle that affixes easily to household taps in order to reduce water use – and thus, waste – by as much as ninety per cent.

We learn about togetherness from those around us in the real world. From their base in Singapore, three generations of the Soh family are revolutionizing the concept of a *kampung* for the twenty-first century. Between their urban farm garden, cooking school and research and development lab-cum-atelier, the house is as much a start-up HQ as it is a family home. Moreover, each family member is deeply connected to an ecosystem of pals, peers and passers-through.

Theirs is a profound, community-focused understanding of togetherness.

Likewise, community is always at the forefront of fashion designer Bubu Ogisi's practice. She works between Lagos, Accra and Nairobi, threading artisanal craftsmanship, recycled materials and stories sourced across the African continent into her rich, nuanced collections. One morning might see her weaving with plastic; by the afternoon, she could be recontextualizing the story of a forgotten kingdom for a new generation. She's fascinated by layers, she explains, 'I take different ingredients from different places and put them together; everything is connected.'

For photographer Sahil Babbar, the idea of togetherness is tied up with that of family. As such, it's divided for him between New Delhi, India – where he was born, and lived until the age of five – and Ontario, Canada, where he grew up thereafter. Unknown though his subjects are to the viewer, in this series about his extended family their presence nods to heritage, ancestry and the subtle and at-once unavoidable connections that bind us all together, wherever we are in the world.

RYET

FÖRNUFTIG

MISTELN

Design by IKEA of Sweden, 2021

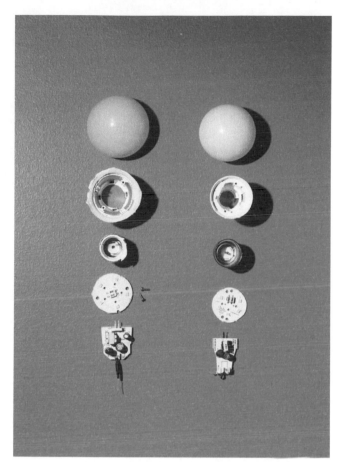

Design by IKEA of Sweden, 2015

RYET IKEA has long believed in the power of collectivity. Especially when it comes to the climate crisis, and the company's ongoing mission to make sustainable living accessible to the many.

In the early 2010s, motivated by the fact that lighting accounts for some fifteen per cent of the world's electricity consumption, Ingvar Kamprad suggested switching all IKEA light bulbs to LED – by far the most energy-efficient option, but also an expensive one.

He set the IKEA development team a Herculean task: to create a high-quality LED bulb for just one euro. They duly set about re-evaluating every element of existing LED offerings in search of ways of lowering prices without affecting standards.

At last, they found a solution: by spending more on higher-quality parts for the LED section of the bulb, other parts of the power supply could be removed, reducing the bulb's final cost to exactly one euro. The result was RYET, an affordable collection of standard bulb fittings, each lasting up to 15,000 hours and consuming approximately eighty-five per cent less energy than incandescent bulbs.

But IKEA didn't stop there. RYET will be replaced with a trailblazing upgrade.

The new bulbs are up to thirty-five per cent more energy efficient than its predecessors, providing 25,000 hours of illumination – around twenty years – and better light quality. The collection comes in many shapes and sizes, includes dimmable options, and costs even less than the other ranges. When put to use by IKEA customers, the new bulb has the potential to save up to 45,000 tonnes of CO_2 per year.

TOGETHERNESS

FÖRNUFTIG Clean air, like clean water, is vital to keeping our bodies healthy. But in spite of this, nine in ten of us breathe in air that exceeds the World Health Organization's guideline limit for pollutants. Worse still, an estimated seven million people die annually, worldwide, as a result of the many illnesses that air pollution can trigger.

While we might imagine that air contamination is largely confined to major cityscapes, studies have found that the air within our homes – both urban and rural – contains a high number of pollutants, from dust to cooking fumes to gas chemicals like formaldehyde.

Propelled by a desire to make clean air accessible to as many people as possible, IKEA set out to develop its sleek yet affordable air purifier, FÖRNUFTIG, which launched in 2020.

A discreet, lightweight rectangular box in black or pale grey, FÖRNUFTIG comes with a filter for particle removal, which is optimized to filter away approximately ninety-nine and a half per cent of smaller airborne particles, such as PM2.5 particles, dust and pollen. A separately sold filter for gas cleaning can also be inserted to target gaseous pollutants like formaldehyde and reduce the odours produced by smoking or cooking.

While creating FÖRNUFTIG, the design team's biggest challenge was to optimize and simplify all of the purifier's intricate technical details to guarantee both low cost and high quality, while ensuring maximum energy efficiency.

Visually the aim was to enable FÖRNUFTIG to blend seamlessly into the home, according to its designer David Wahl. It can hang vertically or horizontally on the wall or stand upright on the floor, while its removable handle allows it to be transported from room to room.

Soon, IKEA will release a new air purifier, STARKVIND, expanding on all that FÖRNUFTIG has already achieved.

Design by David Wahl, 2020

Design by IKEA of Sweden, Altered, soon

MISTELN According to The World Wide Fund for Nature, around seventy-five per cent of the world's population will be affected by water scarcity by 2025. Yet many of us use far more water than we need to: Europeans use an average of 150 litres of water daily, Americans even more.

At home, water wastage often comes down to bad habits; leaving the tap running while cleaning your teeth, for instance, equates to up to twelve litres going down the drain per minute.

Keen to be part of the water scarcity solution, IKEA began introducing water-saving taps and showers into their bathroom and kitchen ranges, but soon recognized an increasing need to develop more extreme water-saving measures, and fast.

In 2016, IKEA sought out the expertise of Swedish innovation company, Altered, who produce transformative water-saving solutions for existing household fittings. The companies joined forces, applying IKEA's design thinking to Altered's patented technology for atomizing water, which gives every droplet its own, more powerful surface, while increasing the speed of flow to ensure maximum 'efficiency' from each drop. The result is MISTELN, a soon-to-be-launched tap adaptor that reduces water usage by over ninety per cent.

Set to retail at five euros, the compact, black nozzle comes with an adaptor kit that means it can be used with the majority of tap fittings, and boasts two settings, mist and spray, depending on how much water you require. The aerator and handle are made from recycled plastic, the inside from reinforced polyamide plastic for durability and hygiene.

It's a small but vital move towards reducing the collective impact of our bad water habits: if the tap is accidentally left running for a minute with MISTELN, it'll use one quarter of a litre of water – a difference of over ninety-seven per cent.

TOGETHERNESS

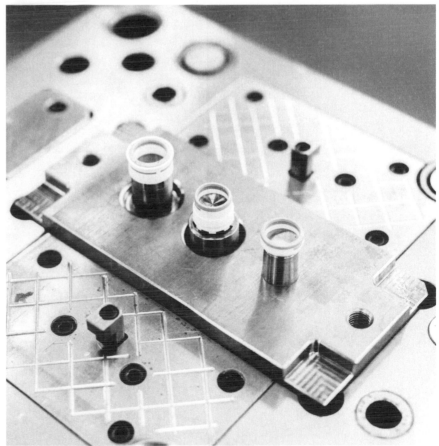

THE SOH FAMILY

HIDDEN WITHIN THE neat suburbs between Singapore's Katong and Siglap districts, the Soh family has created a unique haven. Calvin and his partner Arlette, their children Eva and Dylan, and matriarch Ng Swee Hiah – 'Mummy Soh' – founded One Kind House together in 2016, when the children were just ten and thirteen years old. Consisting of an urban farm garden, a cooking school, a research and development lab-cum-atelier and private family quarters, the space is at once a start-up HQ, a *kampung*, or traditional village kitchen, and a family home. In a densely populated city-state where only five per cent of the population now resides in 'landed' houses, the Sohs are exploring, through their home and their family, what it means to keep the *kampung* spirit alive in the twenty-first century.

TZ: **How did One Kind House start?**

CS: My grandparents bought this house in 1969. They had twelve kids, and my mum was the eldest. I grew up in a four-bedroom Housing Development Board flat for a while, but my mum bought this house from her siblings in 1985, after her parents passed on, and she kept it to fulfil a promise to them. At that time, everyone in this neighbourhood used to grow their own stuff; there were chickens and ducks everywhere. We had a *kampung* around us. Now, we have apartment blocks.

My mum retired around the time I decided to become a stay-at-home dad. Arlette and I put all our money and a lot of effort into figuring out, 'What is the home for the future, for both my mum and our kids? What is retirement in this new world? What is education?' I knew my mum's skills; she could teach, she could cook, she could plant. For the kids, we knew we had to prepare them for a drastically different future to the one we had been prepared for at their age. We thought a lot about what values we needed to focus on. We decided that as long as they could pass their exams at school, they would gain more value from coming here and hosting dinners with mum and spending time at the R&D lab upstairs.

TZ: **The family doesn't live here full time?**

CS: Think of it as a family office. We have an apartment five minutes away. Currently, we all live there, except for Uncle Ng Yak Whee, Mummy Soh's brother. We all spend at least four days a week here.

TZ: **What are your favourite spaces in the house?**

DS: I like the smaller table, where we play poker as a family. And the front room, where Mama [Mummy Soh] has her daybed I sit and play my guitar with her.

Words TÜRKÜ ZORLUTUNA
Photography JULIANA TAN

ES: My favourite room is upstairs, with my sewing machines. When I'm focused on something, I'm kind of in my zone, I'm in a flow state.

ATS: One of mine is upstairs in the R&D lab, because when Eva and Dylan are discovering new things, I like being on that journey with them. The other place is the turntable downstairs. We constantly play records that we've collected on our travels, it's a key part of what makes One Kind House: food, culture, music.

TZ: **Mummy Soh, what's your favourite space in the house?**

MS: The back garden and the kitchen.

TZ: **Like mother, like son! I notice there's a difference in the style of growing between the front and the back gardens; Calvin's and Dylan's garden in the front is very neatly sectioned, but the back is more wild.**

CS: This is how she grows: whatever she chops, she takes the seeds and throws it in the garden, and it grows.

MS: That's why there's so much chilli out there!

TZ: **I'd love to hear about the cooking classes and dinners.**

CS: People arrive as strangers, but they leave as lifelong friends. One of the key things is that there are a lot of ideas exchanged. This is what building a twenty-first-century *kampung* is all about, rather than making a *kampung* that is focused on creating a self-sufficient, siloed collective. We need the exchange of ideas to be a key part of what 'community' means, to ensure that small communities, as a way of living, survive.

TZ: **This is not your typical family set-up, especially in Singapore.**

CS: It was a bit lonely at the beginning. Some of the parents that come here, they've said they liked it, but they

wondered how we knew we were doing the right thing. We don't! But there are a lot of these inter-connected dots that come together and seem to make sense, they give us hope that we're heading in the right direction. We work on family projects all together. Take our current project.

DS: It is the world's first modular, Lego-like hydroponic system. It's intended for apartments, most of which aren't designed for urban farming. We're partnering with nursing homes and social housing projects to provide more access to growing for lower-income families and, especially, the elderly.

TZ: **So, It's centred around creating a meaningful retirement for Singapore's ageing population?**

CS: That is a big issue here in Singapore. My dad worked really hard to retire at sixty, he looked forward to It his whole life. But when he and my mum both retired, they didn't know what to do with themselves, because all their generation could think about was putting food on the table. Nowadays, we all talk about, 'What's your *ikigai*, what's your purpose?' Back then, that wasn't really considered.

Within six months of retiring, my father was diag-nosed with stage four colon cancer. By sixty-three, it was over. That's why I did what I could to stop working younger, despite the financial implications. I might die at sixty-two, but I won't have that regret. But then again, I could live to 100 ... [he looks at Eva and Dylan] Then I'll be a pain in your ass.

DS: And then I'll regret it! [laughs]

TZ: **Dylan and Eva, do you notice some difference between your family life and that of your friends?**

ES: We have a community that I don't think most peo-ple have at the age of fifteen. Usually, It's limited to their friends and immediate family. We're part of a much wider community and so we understand ecosys-tems – I'm not talking about plants, I'm talking about people. Here, we're always exchanging ideas, we're always barter trading. We have a deep connection to our ecosystem.

'We're always exchanging ideas, we're always barter trading. We have a deep connection to our ecosystem.'

— EVA SOH

TZ: **Mummy Soh, if there was one life lesson that you could pass on to your grandchildren about what makes a good *kampung*, what would it be?**

MS: Family togetherness. And food,

Ritual:
The Soh family gathers around the dining table

'**THE FRONT GARDEN** and the dining room are one,' Calvin Soh explains, gesturing towards the garden which abuts One Kind House. 'Everything we eat in here, we grow out there.' In fact, when the Soh family renovated the building several years ago, they redesigned the layout to make the dining area its central space, with a view that runs unobstructed from the front door all the way through to the dining area at the back. Above it, a triple-height ceiling frames the space, like a church.

At the centre of the room sits a 4-metre-long (13-foot-long) table, made from salvaged Australian railway jarrah wood which is 200 years old. It is the centrepiece of their family life. 'Let me tell you the story of this table,' Calvin continues. 'One of our friends was dating a Swiss artist who made this table for their house. After they broke up, she wanted to get rid of it, but what do you do with a 4-metre (13-foot) table? So, she offered it to us.

We just paid for the shipping, and hosted her and her friends for a dinner party as a trade. I didn't realize, until it arrived, just how perfect it really was. So, this table is now where we sit around, every day, and we discuss as a family: what has caught our attention today? What are the problems out in the world, and how can we solve them?'

It's thanks to this family ritual that Calvin's daughter, Eva Soh, started a series of women's empowerment projects at the age of fourteen, and that his son, Dylan Soh, began designing One Kind Block, a modular hydroponic growing system intended to create access to growing for lower-income families. One Kind House sits at the heart of an ever-growing ecosystem – and at the core of this ecosystem sits this table.

Words TÜRKÜ ZORLUTUNA
Photography JULIANA TAN

Photo Essay: Sahil Babbar

WARMTH, ACCEPTANCE, CURIOSITY, restraint – the ties that bind us to our relations take on a different character at different times. In this photo series, Sahil Babbar captures his extended family in their homes between New Delhi, India, and Ontario, Canada, with intimacy, sensitivity and nuance. In each carefully constructed tableau, every pose, knick-knack and outfit detail hints at a rich and complex web of inter-familial relationships, calling to mind the invisible threads that connect us all.

BUBU

OGISI

TOGETHERNESS

FOR BUBU OGISI, the art of garment-making is about much more than simply producing clothing. It requires intention, time and ritual. It's a spiritual, meditative process – the duration of which imbues each piece she creates with a unique magic.

The designer was born in Nigeria and brought up between London and Lagos, and studied fashion at the École Supérieure des Arts et Techniques de la Mode in Paris. On her return to Africa, she crossed the continent, travelling from the West to Kenya in the East, in order to explore a craft culture which has women at the centre of it.

Her brand I.AM.ISIGO was founded in 2009, fusing African culture with an audacious yet minimal design aesthetic and a versatile and fashion-forward DNA – and always producing as little waste as possible. Now, she divides her time between Lagos, Nairobi and Accra in Ghana, aligning elements from the sartorial and craft culture of each country. In this, her work epitomizes togetherness, as expressed through textiles.

When we meet in the workshop, Bubu wears a warm coat made from three attached suit jackets, a hat whose style has long been associated with Mobutu Sese Seko, two dresses and faux-fur slides – all in varying shades of brown – to shield herself from the Nairobi winter. Our setting is Beacon of Hope, a non-profit which, since 2002, has trained over 3,120 women in crafts and other skills to help them escape the cycle of poverty. Together we looked at samples of past and near-future collections among the looms, design tables and tapestry rooms. I found her pondering a huge sheet of translucent blue plastic.

AO: **So, are you going to cut this up and weave it?**

BO: I prefer doing it in patches, so that there's no waste involved. I like everything to be left naturally so that there's this raw detailing. That's I.AM.ISIGO, you know? I take different ingredients from different places and put them together; everything is connected.

Everybody, everything is made of layers. We start from something, and then we keep on evolving. Different cultures have different layers, which have affected each of us differently. Different personalities, different backgrounds. I always want to send an intentional message with an outfit or a textile, or anything I'm creating, even if it's not in your face – if you know, you know.

AO: **Is this a bathing sponge?**

BO: Yeah [chuckles]. It's so cool! I thought it'd make such a nice bag. And you can have a little shower with it ... But not really. It's 'multifunctional'. These are also

Words AWUOR ONYANGO
Photography MAGANGA MWAGOGO

LIFE VISIT

TOGETHERNESS

AO: I can see a link between this idea and your efforts to rescue plastic from the limited ideas we have about it. A material can shape an empire or era. For us, unfortunately, it's plastic – and we don't know what to do with it.

BO: We don't know what to do with hemp either. We're just learning. One of my weaver's grandsons did his thesis in school on using it for building blocks for housing, for fabrics, for wood, for everything. She was so open to the idea. Most people would be like 'oh, I can't touch that!'

AO: In a time when so much is done by AI or machine, you're building a community of human beings to do it.

BO: The art of garment-making, for me, is about way more than just volumes. I think it's really cool to use your hands for a spiritual, meditative process, as opposed to giving the work to a machine. Most of the craftspeople are women here. In West Africa it's mostly men, even on the loom. It's said that women can't sit on the machine, or there won't be any luck. It was nice to see how the story changed on the other side of the continent. To really understand the truth about the patriarchy behind tapestry in West Africa, as opposed to what's happening in East Africa.

AO: Did you make your last collection here too?

BO: Yes. Shifra makes my jackets, and sometimes dresses. Anastacia is the lady on the loom. Raya makes trousers and skirts.

For this collection, I wanted to create something that's subtle and soft, but still very layered. It's inspired by how textures can be soothing and healing at the same time. I also like to revisit ideas and expand on them, so after this process we will mix hemp and plastic to show that coexistence of worlds, of natural and synthetic fibres.

Plastic is never going to go anywhere. We have to deal with that, to face reality. I want to find a balance between those worlds – the synthetic and the natural, in terms of fashion waste.

AO: When does your design process start?

BO: Apart from reading and doing research, I like to travel to different African countries, and see what the connection is between them. Learn about new histories, new stories. That inspires me to create. The first part of the process has to do with travelling and movement.

carrier bags I got in Senegal and in Kenya. We're going to turn them into trousers.

AO: *Gunias* and plastics, are those the layers you're focusing on for this collection?

BO: We're weaving with hemp and cotton, and probably a little bit of plastic also. We're opening up people's minds to new eco-innovative designs. So, we're using red, yellow, blue and the natural colour of the hemp too. The idea is based on the land of Kush.

AO: Kush, the empire?

BO: Exactly! I'm reading this book, *The Lost Cities of Africa*, which details different events from the Kush empire, the Moors, the Yoruba empire, the Benin empire. But in particular linking the Kush empire to the history around hemp as a material, and its use for healing and medicinal purposes.

AO: **What inspires you?**

BO: I usually ride around on a *boda boda* [a motorcycle taxi] so I can see things face to face. The littlest things inspire me: the lady selling food on the side of the road, the *kanjo* workers. I love shopping and people watching at the market, seeing how they mix colours. It's very raw. And I like watching documentaries – about lost cities of Africa, the history of textiles, nature documentaries, different dictators. I'm really obsessed with dictators.

AO: **There's something about how dictators create a personality that makes their fashion ...**

BO: ... dIfferent! I find them really entertaining, because they are delusional, but they have this sense of dressing that's quite unique, and very specific to their personality at the same time.

'I take different ingredients from different places and put them together; everything is connected.'

— **BUBU OGISI**

CONTRIBUTORS

MOHAMAD ABDOUNI, Lebanon
Mohamad Abdouni is a Lebanese photographer, film-maker and visual artist based in Beirut and Istanbul, and the founder of *Cold Cuts* magazine. On pages 121–8, he captures activist and restaurateur Kamal Mouzawak in his Beirut apartment.

SAHIL BABBAR, Canada
Sahil Babbar is a New Delhi-born, Toronto-based photographer and filmmaker, who is interested in the limits of language and the line between the real and the imagined. His powerful photo essay on pages 233–9 zooms in on family connections.

EMMA CAPPS, Mexico
Emma Capps is a writer and editor working in London and Mexico City, across art, culture and fashion. She interviews the eco-conscious Rodriguez-Martin family on pages 165–9.

MATTHEW DONALDSON, UK
Matthew Donaldson is a photographer and filmmaker, based in London, whose work focuses on portraiture, still-life and fashion photography. See his playful response to the theme of food on pages 113–19.

DEVASHISH GAUR, India
Devashish Gaur is a Delhi-based photographer and multidisciplinary artist, interested in ideas of home, identity and intimacy. He documents climate change activist Ridhima Pandey at home on pages 41–8.

JADE GEORGE, Lebanon
Jade George is a writer and editor based in Beirut and Athens, and one of the co-founders of *Art and Then Some*. Read her interview with entrepreneur, restaurateur and activist Kamal Mouzawak on pages 125–9.

JULIEN T. HAMON, France
Julien T. Hamon is a photographer based in Paris, whose work spans portraiture, fashion and documentary photography. On pages 179–91, he turns his lens on Jean-Charles Leuvrey, founder of Hotel Radio Paris.

BRIANNA HOLT, USA
Brianna Holt is a writer and author based in New York and Malmö, whose work spans societal change, music and cultural analysis. Turn to pages 143–50 for her interview with artist, designer and skateboarder Alexis Sablone.

TAKASHI HOMMA, Japan
Takashi Homma is a Tokyo-based photographer well known for his landscape photography and portraiture. On pages 59–71, he documents Midori Shintani, head gardener of the Tokachi Millennium Forest.

JOANNA KAWECKI, Japan
Joanna Kawecki is an Australia-born writer and editor and the founder of *Ala Champ* magazine. She lives in Tokyo, where she specializes in design and architecture. Read her interview with Midori Shintani on pages 63–70.

ARI MARCOPOULOS, USA
Ari Marcopoulos is an Amsterdam-born artist, filmmaker and photographer living in New York, whose oeuvre includes portraits, street scenes and landscapes. On pages 139–51, he shoots Alexis Sablone at home and in her Brooklyn studio.

MO MFINANGA, USA
Mahmoud 'Mo' Mfinanga is a Detroit-born artist based in Brooklyn and Los Angeles. His output spans photography, writing and art direction. He captures fashion designer-turned-activist Ron Finley tending to his garden on pages 99–111.

MAGANGA MWAGOGO, Kenya
Maganga Mwagogo is a Nairobi-based photographer and filmmaker, working primarily in the realms of documentary and fashion. On pages 241–8, he photographs fashion designer Bubu Ogisi.

BRIGITTE NIEDERMAIR, Italy
Brigitte Niedermair is an artist and photographer based in Merano. See her restorative photo essay, made from her studio window, on pages 153–9.

AWUOR ONYANGO, Kenya

Awuor Onyango is a Nairobi-based writer and multidisciplinary artist, whose practice is concerned with claiming public space disallowed to people considered Black and femme. They interview Bubu Ogisi on pages 245–9.

KEVIN E.G. PERRY, USA

Kevin E.G. Perry is a Los Angeles-based writer, who specializes in the fields of music, film and culture. On pages 103–10, he interviews Ron Finley from the empty swimming pool that houses part of his verdant garden.

GUEORGUI PINKHASSOV, Russia

Gueorgui Pinkhassov is a Moscow-based photographer best known for his vivid art reportage. He documents the Leven family at home in their Khimki apartment on pages 81–8.

BARBARA PROBST, Germany

Barbara Probst is a photographer and visual artist living in Munich and New York. Her photographic work spans street scenes, still lifes and fashion imagery. On pages 33–9, she delivers a captivating photo essay, fracturing a single moment in time.

GAUTAMI REDDY, India

Gautami Reddy is a New Delhi-based writer and the director of digital and communications for India Art Fair. Read her interview with Ridhima Pandey on pages 45–9.

PIA RIVEROLA, Mexico

Pia Riverola is a Barcelona-born photographer based in Los Angeles and Mexico City, focused on fashion, still-life, landscape and architectural photography. On pages 161–8, she fixes her lens on the Rodriguez-Martin family in Guadalajara, Mexico.

CASPER SEJERSEN, Denmark

Casper Sejersen is a Copenhagen-based photographer, whose practice is centred around fashion, film and fine art. See his documentation of artist Misaki Kawai and her family in their new home on pages 201–8.

LIV SIDDALL, Netherlands

Liv Siddall is a writer, editor and podcaster based in London and Amsterdam, who specializes in design, music, art and culture. Discover her interview with artist Misaki Kawai and her family on pages 205–9.

THOMAS SITO, Indonesia

Makassar-born photographer Thomas Sito predominantly creates fashion and still-life photographs. On pages 19–31, he captures the world of Bali-based designer Elora Hardy and her family.

JULIANA TAN, Singapore

Juliana Tan is a Singapore-based photographer and director, whose passion lies in portraiture and long-form picture essays. Peruse her photographs of the collectively minded Soh family on pages 219–31.

BANDANA TEWARI, Indonesia

Bandana Tewari is an India-born, Bali-based fashion and lifestyle journalist and sustainability activist. Read her interview with Elora Hardy on pages 23–30.

HAYDÉE TOUITOU, France

Haydée Touitou is a Paris-based poet, writer, journalist and editor, and one of the co-founders of *The Skirt Chronicles*. She interviews Jean-Charles Leuvrey on his barge just outside the city, on pages 183–90.

LIAM SIELSKI WATERS, UK

Liam Sielski Waters is a London-based image-maker and art director, whose practice ranges from spatial design and product visualization to branding and conceptual art. On pages 73–9, he reimagines the theme of space as an illusory CGI landscape.

DAISY WOODWARD, Germany

Daisy Woodward is a writer and editor based in Berlin, where she specializes in art, culture, fashion and film. She interviews the Leven family on pages 85–9.

HUGO YU, USA

Hugo Yu is a Shanghai-born, New York-based photographer, whose work ranges from documentary street photography to carefully crafted studio work. On pages 193–9, he creates a series of whimsical still-life images inspired by the theme of play.

TÜRKÜ ZORLUTUNA, Singapore

Türkü Zorlutuna is a Singapore-based brand and communications strategist, whose expertise lies in food culture and sustainability. She interviews the Soh family on pages 223–30.

INDEX

PICTURE CREDITS

ACKNOWLEDGEMENTS

The Publisher would like to thank the following people for their contribution to the book:

Fernanda Anaya, Hilary Bird, Sara Borgström, Richard Clack, Adela Cory, Lars Dafnäs, DoBeDo Represents, Linda Edevik, Marcus Engman, Guillaume Fabiani, Therese Gerdman, Sophie Gladstone, Holly Hay, IKEA Marketing & Communication, IKEA Museum, IKEA of Sweden, Ehlén Johansson, Nike Karlsson, Oskar Krona, Petter Kukacka, Linda Lindestam, Magnum Photos, Marie Lundström, Amanda Mackie, João Mota, Tony Nilsson, Rita Peres Pereira, Jennifer Permata, Mattias Rexare, Kim Scott, Lena Simonsson-Berge, Maisie Skidmore, Seetal Solanki, Rikard Uddenberg, Vivek Vadoliya, Maria Vinka, Elaine Ward, Jonathan Whale, Daisy Woodward, DK Woon, Linda Worbin, Regina Zinnatova.

Phaidon Press Limited
2 Cooperage Yard
London, E15 2QR

Phaidon Press Inc.
65 Bleecker Street
New York, NY 10012

phaidon.com

First published 2022

ISBN 978 1 83866 489 3

A CIP catalogue record for this book is available from
the British Library and the Library of Congress.

Commissioning Editor: Emilia Terragni
Project Editor: Kim Scott
Editor: Maisie Skidmore
Creative Strategist: DK Woon
Contributing Writer: Daisy Woodward

Creative Director: Petter Kukacka
Art Director/Designer: Oskar Krona
Artworker: Rita Peres Pereira

Photo Editor: Holly Hay
Photo Producer: Sophie Gladstone

Production: Elaine Ward, Adela Cory, Amanda Mackie

Printed in Germany